Key Concepts
in
American History

Colonialism

Set Contents

Key Concepts in American History

Abolitionism

Colonialism

Expansionism

Federalism

Industrialism

Internationalism

Isolationism

Nationalism

Progressivism

Terrorism

Key Concepts
in
American History

Colonialism

Darrell J. Kozlowski

Jennifer L. Weber, Ph.D.
General Editor
University of Kansas

CHELSEA HOUSE
PUBLISHERS
An imprint of Infobase Publishing

Key Concepts in American History: Colonialism

DEVELOPED, DESIGNED, AND PRODUCED BY DWJ BOOKS LLC

Chelsea House
An imprint of Infobase Publishing
132 West 31st Street
New York NY 10001

Library of Congress Cataloging-in-Publication Data

Kozlowski, Darrell J.
    Colonialism / Darrell Kozlowski ; Jennifer L. Weber, general editor.
    p.   cm. – (Key concepts in American history)
    Includes bibliographical references and index.
    ISBN 978-1-60413-217-5 (hardcover)
1. United States—Economic conditions—To 1865—Encyclopedias, Juvenile. 2. United States—Economic conditions—1865–1918—Encyclopedias, Juvenile. 3. Industrial revolution—United States—History—19th century—Encyclopedias, Juvenile. 4. Industrial revolution—United States—History—20th century—Encyclopedias, Juvenile. I. Weber, Jennifer L., 1962– II. Title. III. Series.
    HC105.M225 2009
    338.097303-dc22
                              2009025283

Chelsea House books are available at special discounts when purchased in bulk quantities for businesses, associations, institutions, or sales promotions. Please call our Special Sales Department in New York at (212)967-8800 or (800)322-8755.

You can find Chelsea House on the World Wide Web at http://www.chelseahouse.com

Cover printed by Bang Printing, Brainerd, MN
Book printed and bound by Bang Printing, Brainerd, MN
Date printed: May 2010
Printed in the United States of America

10 9 8 7 6 5 4 3 2 1

This book is printed on acid-free paper and contains 30 percent postconsumer recycled content.

Acknowledgments
pp. 9, 14, 18, 28, 36, 40, 52, 68, 69, 86: The Granger Collection, New York; p. 90: Library of Congress, Prints and Photographs Division.

Contents

List of Illustrations

Photos

Maps

Reader's Guide
to Colonialism

The list that follows is provided as an aid to readers in locating articles on the big topics or themes in **American Colonial History.** The Reader's Guide arranges all of the A to Z entries in *Key Concepts in American History: Colonialism* according to these **9 key concepts** of the social studies curriculum: **Colonies**; **Economics and Trade**; **European Nations**; **Explorers and Conquerors**; **Government**; **Native Americans**; **People and Society**; **Religion**; and **Wars and Battles**. Some articles appear in more than one category, helping readers to see the links between topics.

Milestones in

After European explorers and adventurers discovered the Americas, colonization throughout the Western Hemisphere increased quickly. European nations hoped to gain power and wealth by sending their people to settle the new lands.

Spain sent the first European **colonists** to the Americas, followed by Portugal. By the mid-1700s, however, Great Britain held the most powerful colonial empire in the Americas.

1325 Aztecs found the city of Tenochtitlán in what is today Mexico.

1440 The Portuguese are the first Europeans to take slaves from Africa.

1488 Bartholomeu Dias reaches the southern tip of Africa.

1492 Christopher Columbus finds the Americas, leading to European colonization of the new lands.

1494 The Treaty of Tordesillas divides the New World between Spain and Portugal.

1497 John Cabot claims the eastern shore of Canada for England, paving the way for later colonization.

1498 Vasco da Gama's fleet reaches the Indian port of Calicut, having found an all-water route to the Indies.

1510 Vasco Nuñez de Balboa establishes the colony of Santa Maria la Antiqua del Darién in what is today Panama.

1513 Balboa is the first European to see the Pacific Ocean.

1513 Juan Ponce de León claims and explores Florida for Spain.

1517 Ferdinand Magellan sets sail to find a sea route to the Indies for Spain.

1519 Hernán Cortés reaches Tenochtitlán, capital of the Aztec empire, on November 12.

1521 The Aztec empire collapses on August 13.

1522 The *Victoria,* one of Magellan's ships, becomes the first ship to circumnavigate the globe.

1523 Spanish conquistador Francisco Pizarro arrives in Peru.

1524 Giovanni da Verrazano claims Newfoundland for France.

1533 The Inca empire is conquered by Spanish conquistadors, leading to Spanish colonization of South America.

1534 Jacques Cartier claims the Gulf of St. Lawrence for France.

1541 Hernando de Soto reaches the Mississippi River on May 8.

1553 Negotiations between the English and the Russians lead to the founding of the Muscovy Company.

1580 Francis Drake becomes the first Englishman to circumnavigate the globe.

1585 Walter Raleigh and his group attempt to colonize Roanoke Island.

Colonialism (1300s-1834)

1587 Virginia Dare is the first English child born in the Americas.

1588 The English navy defeats the Spanish Armada.

1602 The Dutch East India Company is founded.

1606 King James I of England grants charters to establish the Virginia Company and the London Company and founds the Plymouth Company.

1607 Jamestown is established by the London Company.

1608 Samuel de Champlain founds Quebec.

1609 Henry Hudson claims New Netherland and begins exploring the Hudson River.

1612 John Rolfe begins growing tobacco in Jamestown.

1619 A Dutch slave-trading ship brings the first Africans to America.

1619 Members of the House of Burgesses meet for the first time in Virginia.

1620 The *Mayflower* reaches Plymouth Rock.

1637 The New Sweden Company is formed.

1638 The New Sweden Company settles New Sweden, or what today is called Delaware.

1643 The New England Confederation is established.

1654 John Casor becomes the first legally recognized slave in the thirteen colonies.

1662 A hereditary slavery law is established in Virginia.

1673 French explorers Jacques Marquette and Louis Joliet set out to explore the Mississippi River.

1682 Robert de La Salle claims Louisiana for France.

1689 The Glorious Revolution removes James II from the English throne.

1705 The Virginia slave codes restrict the movement of blacks.

1728 Vitus Bering sails the Bering Strait.

1750 Thomas Walker discovers the Cumberland Gap, leading to easier settlement of the land west of the Appalachian Mountains.

1754 The French and Indian War begins.

1763 The Treaty of Paris is signed, ending the French and Indian War.

1763 King George III issues the Proclamation of 1763.

1799 Czar Paul I grants a charter to the Russian American Company.

1807 Great Britain outlaws the African slave trade.

1834 Britain outlaws slave ownership within its colonies.

Preface

The United States was founded on ideas. Those who wrote the U.S. Constitution were influenced by ideas that began in Europe: reason over religion, human rights over the rights of kings, and self-governance over tyranny. Ideas, and the arguments over them, have continued to shape the nation. Of all the ideas that influenced the nation's founding and its growth, 10 are perhaps the most important and are singled out here in an original series—KEY CONCEPTS IN AMERICAN HISTORY. The volumes bring these concepts to life, *Abolitionism, Colonialism, Expansionism, Federalism, Industrialism, Internationalism, Isolationism, Nationalism, Progressivism,* and *Terrorism.*

These books examine the big ideas, major events, and influential individuals that have helped define American history. Each book features three sections. The first is an overview of the concept, its historical context, the debates over the concept, and how it changed the history and growth of the United States. The second is an encyclopedic, A-to-Z treatment of the people, events, issues, and organizations that help to define the "-ism" under review. Here, readers will find detailed facts and vivid histories, along with referrals to other books for more details about the topic.

Interspersed throughout the entries are many high-interest features: "History Speaks" provides excerpts of documents, speeches, and letters from some of the most influential figures in American history. "History Makers" provides brief biographies of key people who dramatically influenced the country. "Then and Now" helps readers connect issues of the nation's past with present-day concerns.

In the third part of each volume, "Viewpoints," readers will find longer primary documents illustrating ideas that reflect a certain point of view of the time. Also included are important government documents and key Supreme Court decisions.

The KEY CONCEPTS series also features "Milestones in. . .," time lines that will enable readers to quickly sort out how one event led to another, a glossary, and a bibliography for further reading.

People make decisions that determine history, and Americans have generated and refined the ideas that have determined U.S. history. With an understanding of the most important concepts that have shaped our past, readers can gain a better idea of what has shaped our present.

Jennifer L. Weber, Ph.D.
Assistant Professor of History, University of Kansas
General Editor

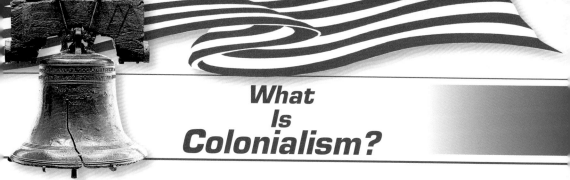

What Is Colonialism?

What is colonialism? It really is a simple concept. Colonialism is the extension of a country's rule to lands beyond its own borders. These "new" lands established by the parent country are called colonies. The colonies may be either **settler colonies,** to which **colonists** move permanently, or **dependencies,** which are governed by the parent country but to which few colonists actually move.

In settler colonies, the native populations and their cultures often are displaced or, sometimes, eliminated. Colonizing nations generally control the natural resources, the labor force, and the markets of a colony. The colonizing power also may attempt to impose the parent country's culture, religion, and language on the native people. Colonialism, then, is a system of direct political, economic, and cultural control by a powerful country over a weaker one.

HISTORY OF COLONIALISM

The history of colonization—the act of extending one's rule to another country—stretches around the globe and across time. The term *colonialism* generally is used to refer to overseas European empires. The history of colonization can be traced back to the ancient Phoenicians and Greeks, however. The Phoenicians, who first settled on the Eastern edge of the Mediterranean Sea, were the major trading power in the Mediterranean region from about 1550 B.C.E. to about 300 B.C.E. They traded with cities in Egypt and Greece and established colonies as far west as present-day Cadiz, Spain.

In ancient Greece, the Greek city-states often established colonies to further trade with foreign countries and thus increase the wealth of the parent city-state. About 30 of the Greek city-states established more than one colony in the Mediterranean region. The most active colonizer was the city-state of Miletus. It set up 90 colonies that stretched across the Mediterranean, from the shores of present-day Turkey in the east to the southern coast of present-day Spain in the west. Several of these colonies were on the northern coast of Africa.

The early Romans often set up colonies to secure new conquests. Early in Rome's history, colonies of Roman citizens secured the two coasts of Italy. The colonists entered each conquered city in military fashion, preceded by flags and banners, and the establishment of the settlement was celebrated with special ceremonies. The Roman colonists were free from taxes and from military service because of their position as colonists in a conquered city.

Later, in the second century B.C.E., colonization became a way for Rome to provide for the poorest of its people. By the first century B.C.E., the Roman rulers were granting land to veteran soldiers to establish colonies. The right to found colonies was taken away from the Roman people by the emperor Julius Caesar (r. 49 B.C.E.–44 B.C.E.). The right to colonize then became an exclusive power of the Roman emperors, who used it mainly to establish military settlements in the provinces of the empire.

EUROPEAN COLONIALISM

Modern European colonialism began in 1415, when Portugal conquered the Muslim port of Ceuta in northern Africa. In the decades that followed, Portuguese explorers sailed south along the west coast of Africa and established trading posts, ports, and forts. This wave of colonialism was led by Portuguese and then Spanish exploration of the coasts of Africa, the Americas, India, and East Asia.

Despite some earlier attempts, it was not until the 1600s that England, France, and the Netherlands successfully established overseas colonies. These nations competed with Spain and Portugal, as well as with each other, for new lands. Ultimately, England became highly successful in North America, establishing thirteen thriving colonies along the Atlantic seaboard.

ENGLAND'S THIRTEEN COLONIES

No one ever took a complete or accurate census of England's colonies on mainland America. By the mid-1700s, however, the thirteen English colonies probably had a total population of about 1,600,000 colonists. About 450,000 of these lived in the New England colonies—Massachusetts, Rhode Island, Connecticut, and New Hampshire. Slightly more than 425,000 lived in the middle colonies—New York, Pennsylvania, New Jersey, and Delaware. More than 700,000 lived in the southern colonies—Maryland, Virginia, North Carolia, South Carolia, and Georgia. The southern colony of Virginia had the largest population, with about 340,000 colonial inhabitants. Georgia, the last colony to be established, was home to fewer than 10,000 colonists.

Blacks accounted for more than 325,000 of the total population of the British colonies. More than 140,000 blacks lived in Virginia, more than 90,000 in the Carolinas, and about 49,000 in Maryland. In the middle colonies, New York had the highest number of blacks—more than 16,000. In New England, the black population was fewer than 13,000.

A Mix of People The English were by far the most numerous of the colonists and made up the dominant group in all of the British colonies. They accounted for about three-fifths of the total white population. Among other national groups, the most numerous were Scots, Scots-Irish, and Germans.

Many Scots welcomed the opportunity to seek a better life in America. The Scots-Irish—descendants of Scots who had settled in Northern Ireland in the early seventeenth century—migrated to America in the late 1600s. The Scots-Irish came because economic difficulties and religious differences became unbearable at home.

Germans settled in Pennsylvania in large numbers, attracted by the advertisements of the colony's founder, William Penn. Other Germans settled in the Hudson River Valley in upper New York. Still others moved southward into the Shenandoah Valley in Virginia and on to the Carolina frontier.

Other non-English groups included the Irish, who settled in all the British colonies, and the Dutch, who lived chiefly in New York and New Jersey. A number of Swedes lived in Delaware. A group of Swiss colonists settled in New Berne, North Carolina, and many French Huguenots—Protestants who escaped religious persecution in their Catholic homeland—settled in South Carolina. Jews, who were persecuted throughout Europe, also sought refuge in British North America.

Social Classes In the earliest colonial days, rough frontier conditions destroyed European social distinctions and classes, as all colonists had to work simply to survive. New social classes eventually appeared later in the colonial era, but the social classes in America were not nearly as rigid as those in Europe.

The colonial upper class included the officials who represented the authority of the British crown. This class also included representatives of the various companies that had founded some of the colonies and the families of the proprietors of other colonies. In the South, the upper class was made up of plantation owners. Wealthy merchants made up the upper class in the middle and New England colonies.

The colonial middle class included skilled workers and tradespeople from the towns, landowning farmers, ministers and other members of the clergy, and lawyers. Poor farmers, workers, and **indentured servants** made up the lower class. At the bottom of society were blacks, both free and enslaved.

Religion in the Colonies Puritan influence dominated in New England. Once in America, the Puritans considered themselves free from the restrictions of England's established Anglican Church, which prevented them from worshipping as they chose. The Puritans gave control of the church to the congregation, and church members elected officers. In the New England colonies, the Puritan churches became very powerful in both religious and secular matters, and people were expected to attend their services. This strict attitude changed in the late 1600s, when Protestants of other faiths began to find religious toleration in the New England colonies.

The middle colonies were the least influenced by English religious groups. Neither the Dutch in New York nor the English Quakers in Pennsylvania tried to control the religion of other settlers. Dutch

The Thirteen Colonies

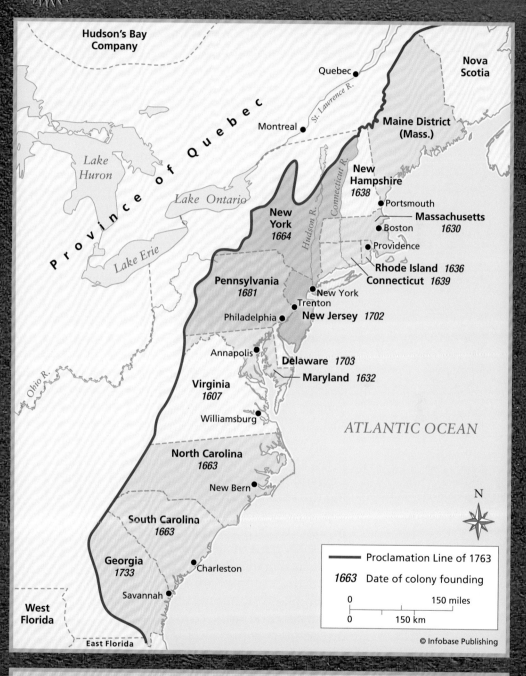

Between 1607 and 1773, English settlers seeking religious freedom and new economic opportunities founded thirteen distinct colonies along the eastern Atlantic Coast. Other settlers came from The Netherlands, Sweden, France, Germany, Scotland, Wales, and Ireland.

Protestants, Presbyterians, Mennonites, Moravians, Lutherans, Quakers, and Catholics lived side by side in the Middle Colonies.

In the southern colonies, the Anglican Church held the same favored position that it held in England. Taxes were paid for the church's support, and royal officials and well-to-do families usually were Anglican. Yet, in the South, the Anglicans lacked the zeal of the New England Puritans, and followers of other faiths lived without fear of persecution.

Steps taken in three colonies led to more religious freedom. In 1649, Maryland's legislature passed the Toleration Act, which provided that no Christians were to be persecuted because of their religious beliefs. In Pennsylvania, William Penn's policy permitted all who acknowledged God to settle there. Penn's policy also made it possible for Jews to find a haven from persecution. Rhode Island was the most liberal of the colonies in religious matters. It followed the principles of its founder, Roger Williams.

Family Life In the early years of colonial settlement, there was little time for any sort of recreation. Working to survive took most of the colonists' time. In some colonies, such as Massachusetts, work, as well as play, was forbidden on Sundays, so that all colonists could attend church services.

In colonial New England, farmers depended on their families to help work the land. Thus, most New England families toiled long hours in the fields during the summer. In the winter, when it became too cold to work outside, the families made furniture, brooms, tools, household utensils, and other needed items. Women of all ages spun wool and flax, wove cloth, and made clothes for their families.

In the colonial South, the great distances between planters' homes tended to discourage social activity in rural areas. To make up for this, the wealthiest planters kept winter residences in cities such as Charleston, South Carolina, and Williamsburg, Virginia. There, the planters and their families enjoyed the winter social season.

Education in the Colonies As the English colonies became more settled, education grew in importance. In New England, close relations between church and state led to the rise of a public school system designed to teach reading and religion. For example, the Massachusetts Public School Law of 1647 required each each town of 50 families or more to support an elelmentary school.

The great variety of religious groups in the middle colonies made the creation of any system of public schools difficult. Furthermore, education was not yet considered a public function. For these reasons, the schools that were established usually were religious schools, maintained by each church for the children of its faith.

PEOPLE SHAPE THE COLONIES

Behind the ideas of colonialism, of course, are the people who settled these lands. The settlers who came to the Americas built each one of the colonies, whether Spanish, English, French, or Dutch, and made each unique. From Spanish explorer Hernán Cortés, we know of the greatness of the Aztec empire in what is today Mexico. Although he was unpopular with colonists, the strict Dutch governor Peter Stuyvesant worked to bring improvements to the colony of New Netherland, today's New York. Englishmen John Smith and John Rolfe saved the fragile Jamestown, Virginia, settlement from perishing and so helped to establish England's first permanent colony in North America.

NATIVE PEOPLES DEFEND THEIR LAND

Huge social, cultural, and religious differences existed between the Native Americans and European settlers. European diseases, for which the native people had no natural immunity, wiped out many tribes, and most colonists viewed the natives as heathens. Tensions between the native peoples and the colonists remained high, especially in the 1600s, as settlers took over even more native land.

In 1634, for example, members of the Narragansett tribe, in what is today Rhode Island, killed an English sea captain. An expedition set sail from Boston under the command of John Endicott to punish the killers. Indeed, Captain Endicott believed he was working God's will against the "savages." After a brief skirmish, the Indians disappeared. Endicott then spent two days burning the empty villages and destroying Indian food supplies.

Captain Endicott next sailed into the area of the native Pequot. The two groups met to establish peace. Endicott, however, distrusted the Pequot. The peace talks broke down, violence erupted, and the colonists destroyed and looted the Indian village.

The furious Pequots directed their anger against the nearest English settlement and besieged Fort Saybrook. In response, the English declared war on the Pequots. In May 1637, English Puritans surrounded a fortified Pequot village. Within an hour, between 400 and 700 native men, women, and children were put to the sword or burned to death as the English torched the village. This massacre broke the tribe's resistance. The colonists then forced a harsh peace, which essentially destroyed the Pequot tribe, on the Native Americans.

Similar tales of escalating violence define the relationship between Native Americans and European settlers. Contact with European colonists resulted in a profound and indelible effect on native culture throughout the Americas. In less than a generation, the world into which the Indians had been born, and for which they had been prepared, vanished forever.

THE COLONIAL LEGACY TODAY

Colonialism shaped the world we live in today. The boundaries of England's thirteen colonies are, in fact, the boundaries for many of today's Eastern Seaboard states. The religious and cultural traditions of our nation have their roots in colonial times. English became the primary language of the United States because the vast majority of the colonists spoke English. Indeed, the United States is a nation of immigrants from around the world.

FURTHER READING

Davis, Kenneth C. *America's Hidden History: Untold Tales of the First Pilgrims, Fighting Women, and Forgotten Founders Who Shaped a Nation.* New York: Collins, 2008.

Hart, Jonathan. *Comparing Empires: European Colonialism from Portuguese Expansion to the Spanish-American War.* New York: Palgrave Macmillan, 2008.

A–C

Appalachian Mountains

Major mountain range in eastern North America. In early colonial times (1607–1750), the Appalachians formed a barrier to British settlement of the land west of the mountains. This mountain range stretches from northeast Alabama, in the southern United States, north into the New England states and eastern Canada. The range is about 1,500 miles (2,400 km) long and between 100 and 300 miles (160 and 480 km) wide.

The Appalachians are made up of several smaller ranges: the White Mountains, the Green Mountains, the Berkshires, and the Blue Ridge among them. At 6,684 ft. (2,037 m), Mount Mitchell in North Carolina is the tallest peak in the Appalachians and the highest point east of the Mississippi River.

During the early years of colonial settlement, thick forests, dense undergrowth, and few passages through the mountains forced the English **colonists** to hug the Atlantic Coast. **Native peoples** populated the land west of the Appalachians, including the area known as the Ohio River Valley. The French, who claimed this area, established a profitable fur trade with the natives but set up few permanent settlements. By the 1750s, however, English settlers were making their way west across the Appalachians to establish forts and settlements in the Ohio River Valley.

Conflict over ownership of the Ohio River Valley soon developed between the British and the French. In 1754, war erupted on the **frontier.**

The Appalachian Mountains stretch from the southeastern United States into Canada. In colonial times, as seen in this wood engraving of an eighteenth-century Virginia settlement, the mountains prevented many settlers from moving westward, away from the Atlantic coast.

The British fought against the French and their Indian **allies.** In North America, this conflict was called the French and Indian War, but it was a part of a wider war that was known in Europe as the Seven Years' War. At this time, England and France fought each other not only in Europe but also throughout the world.

Battles were fought throughout the Ohio River Valley and in French Canada. The fighting in North America ended in 1760, when the French surrendered the city of Montreal, Canada, to the British. Peace was finally established in 1763 with the signing of the Treaty of Paris. As a result of the war, the French lost almost all of their lands in North America. The British gained Canada and the rich lands of the Ohio River Valley.

PROCLAMATION OF 1763

After the Treaty of Paris of 1763 ended the French and Indian War, British colonists hoped to continue establishing settlements in the Ohio River Valley. Quickly, however, the British settlers came into conflict with the Native Americans who lived in the region. As an attempt to maintain peace between the colonists and the Native Americans, the British king, George III (r. 1760–1820), issued the Proclamation of 1763. With this proclamation, the British government tried to prevent colonists from settling west of the Appalachian Mountains by reserving the Ohio River Valley for native peoples. The colonists, however, resented being told that they could not settle in the region. The Proclamation of 1763 was one factor, among many, that ultimately led to the American Revolution (1775–1783).

See also: England; France; French and Indian War; New England; New France; Proclamation of 1763; Thirteen Colonies.

Aztec Empire

Once-powerful Native American empire located in what is today central Mexico. In the early 1500s, the Aztec empire fell to Spanish explorers. It is probable that the **native peoples** who became known as the Aztec slowly **migrated** south (from what is now the southwestern United States) in the sixth century C.E. to the area where Mexico City is today. Over time, these people prospered.

According to a native legend, in 1323, the people saw a vision of an eagle, perched on a cactus, clutching a serpent in its talons. The people interpreted this symbol as showing them where to build a city. In 1325, the Aztec founded the city of Tenochtitlán on a small, swampy island in Lake Texcoco. Tenochtitlán grew to be a vast city and became the capital of the Aztec civilization.

By the early 1400s, the Aztec had joined with the people of two neighboring cities. The Aztec and their **allies** then began a century of conquest. By 1500, the Aztec were the most powerful group in the region, and Tenochtitlán became the center of a mighty empire. This vast empire was held together by Aztec military power. The Aztec demanded **tribute,** in money or slaves, from those they conquered.

AZTEC LIFE

Leading the Aztec society was the emperor, who ruled with the help of powerful nobles. The noble class was made up of members of the royal family and military and religious leaders. Soldiers and craft workers made up another social class. The two lowest classes were farmers and slaves.

The Aztec economy was based on **agriculture.** Aztec farmers developed *chinampas*, rich plots of farmland reclaimed from swampy areas. *Chinampas* were artificial islands made from piles of marsh plants taken from the lake bottom. **Irrigation** and the addition of lake mud kept the *chinampas* fertile. Farming year-round, Aztec farmers grew a **surplus** of food. The extra food was used to feed the craft workers, soldiers, and nobility.

Religion was very important to the Aztec and was ever present in their lives. A **polytheistic** people, they believed it was essential to please their many gods because the gods controlled everything in the peoples' lives. To satisfy their gods, the Aztec made repeated sacrifices, both animal and human. At the height of their power, the Aztec may have sacrificed thousands of people each year.

Aztec architects built huge, pyramid-like temples and grand palaces. Aztec craft workers produced pottery, jewelry, sculpture, and other works of art. The Aztec also developed a system of writing and a complex, 365-day calendar based on the movement of the sun and the stars. The Aztec reached the height of their power by the early 1500s.

FALL OF THE AZTEC EMPIRE

After Christopher Columbus's voyages of discovery to the Caribbean area, Spain sent hundreds of troops to the region in search of gold and other precious materials. One **conquistador,** Hernán Cortés, arrived on the island of Hispaniola—present-day Haiti and the Dominican Republic—in 1504. Hearing rumors of great wealth in the land known as Mexico, Cortés put together an expedition to search for this treasure. In 1519, he reached the Yucatan peninsula with 110 sailors, 550 soldiers, 16 horses, and a few cannons. From the coast, Cortés and his army began to march inland.

Messengers brought the news of the arrival of these strangers to the Aztec emperor, Moctezuma II. The messengers described fantastic animals with two heads and six legs. Because the Aztec had never seen horses, a man riding on horseback appeared to be some strange, new beast. Hearing descriptions of the Spanish and their leader, Moctezuma thought that Cortés was the Aztec god Quetzalcoatl. According to Aztec legend, this ancient god had left Mexico but had promised to return one day as a bearded, fair-skinned man.

As Cortés made his way inland, he learned that many of the non-Aztec people in the area hated the oppressive rule of the Aztec. Through interpreters, Cortés made allies with these people. As he got closer to Tenochtitlán, he sent word that he would like to meet the Aztec ruler and see his capital city. Moctezuma was unsure what to do. Finally, he decided to offer the Spanish gold and other gifts, in the hope that they would take the gifts and leave Mexico. The gods, after all, were terrible beings, and Moctezuma hoped that this one would go away before he and his followers did something horrible to the Aztec people.

When Cortés saw the gold and other treasures that the emperor was offering, he became more determined

A–C

to visit the Aztec capital and gain even greater riches. Cortés and his men started marching to Tenochtitlán. As they approached, Moctezuma, still hoping to bribe them to stay away, continued to send the Spanish gifts. Cortés and his men reached Tenochtitlán on November 12, 1519. When they arrived, they found a huge city with a population of more than 300,000. Indeed, the city was larger than any city in Europe at that time.

Moctezuma, although still fearful of Cortés and his army, invited them to stay in the imperial palace. This proved to be a deadly mistake. As soon as Cortés and his men were in the palace they arrested Moctezuma, claiming that he had ordered an attack on the Spanish. Safe within the palace, and with the emperor as hostage, Cortés needed only a few men to defend his new stronghold.

Last Days of Moctezuma For the next few months, Moctezuma was kept a prisoner in the imperial palace. He tried to please Cortés by erecting statues of the Virgin Mary. Moctezuma even converted to Christianity to please Cortés and swore allegiance to the Spanish king, Charles V.

Moctezuma's attempts to gain favor with Cortés and the Spanish worked at first. He was allowed to continue serving as ruler, even though he had little power. The situation changed in April 1520, however, after Cortés left Tenochtitlán to confront rival Spanish forces that had come from Cuba to claim Mexico's riches. While Cortés was gone, his fellow conquistadors killed more than 3,000 Aztec when the Spanish mistook an Aztec religious festival for a revolt.

Enraged by the killings, the Aztec people of Tenochtitlán rose up against the Spaniards, who had barricaded themselves inside the imperial palace. On July 1, 1520, the Spanish sent Moctezuma outside the palace to calm the mobs. Instead of listening to Moctezuma, however, the people threw stones at him. Knocked unconscious, the Aztec emperor died within two weeks.

Collapse of the Aztec Fighting between the Spanish and the peoples of Mexico continued for several months. With his native allies, Cortés attacked and burned Tenochtitlán, destroying the city. In addition, new diseases brought by the Spanish caused the deaths of untold numbers of Aztec. The Aztec empire collapsed on August 13, 1521. Cortés and the Spaniards soon overran all of central Mexico and claimed its riches for Spain.

See also: **The Diversity of Native America** in the "Viewpoints" section; Native Americans; Spain.

FURTHER READING

Alonso, Roberto Velesco, *et al. The Aztec Empire*. New York: Guggenheim Museum, 2004.

Saunders, Nicholas J., and Tony Allan. The *Aztec Empire: Excavating the Past*. Portsmouth, N.H.: Heinemann Library, 2004.

Balboa, Vasco Nuñez de (1475–1519)

Spanish explorer considered the first European to see the Pacific Ocean after crossing the **Isthmus** á la Panama. Born in 1475 in the Spanish town of Jerez de los Caballeros, Balboa set out on his voyage to the Americas in 1500.

HISTORY MAKERS
Hernán Cortés (1485–1547)

The conquistador Hernán Cortés, who toppled the mighty Aztec empire in 1521, was born in the Spanish city of Medellín to a minor noble family. As a young man, he decided to make his fortune in the Americas. He arrived on the island of Hispaniola in 1504 and at first settled down to become a farmer. Soon, however, a desire for gold and adventure led him to join an expedition of explorers that took over much of the island of Cuba. His reward of land and mines in Cuba made Cortés a wealthy man. In addition, Diego Velázquez de Cuellar, the new governor of Cuba, made Cortés his private secretary and appointed him mayor of Santiago, a city on the southern coast of Cuba.

In 1518, Cortés made plans to leave Cuba and sail to Mexico in search of gold and glory. He landed in Mexico in February 1519. Along the way, he acquired the services of two valuable interpreters. One of the interpreters, Jerónimo de Aguilar, was a Franciscan priest who had been a member of an earlier Spanish expedition and had lived among Mexico's native people. Through Aguilar, Cortés was able to speak with Indians who spoke Mayan. The other interpreter was a young Indian woman whom the Spanish called Marina. She spoke both Mayan and Nahuatl, the language of the Aztec.

Hearing stories of the great wealth of Tenochtitlán, Cortés made his way to that city, the Aztec capital. Along the way, Cortés made allies of many of the Indian groups ruled by the Aztec, and he persuaded many of these people to join his march. By the time he reached Tenochtitlán in late 1519, he had thousands of Indian allies. By the summer of 1521, Cortés and his army had conquered the Aztec.

A–C

Balboa joined the expedition of Rodrigo de Bastidas, who was to bring back gold and other riches to King Ferdinand and Queen Isabella. In 1501, Balboa and the expedition explored the eastern coast of present-day Panama and northern South America. Because the men soon realized that they did not have enough manpower, food, or supplies to start a colony, however, they sailed to the island of Hispaniola. There, the penniless Balboa tried to make a living as a farmer, but he was unsuccessful.

ESCAPE TO CENTRAL AMERICA

In 1509, to escape his creditors in Hispaniola, Balboa hid with his dog in a barrel and stowed away on a ship bound for Panama. In Panama, Balboa joined a small settlement known as San Sabastián de Urabá, which had been founded a few years earlier. Unfortunately, San Sabastián de Urabá was established in an area with poor soil, which made farming difficult. In addition, the **native peoples** of the region were hostile and frequently attacked the settlement.

The Spanish adventurer Vasco Nuñez de Balboa established the first European settlement on the American continent. He was also the first European to see the Pacific Ocean, which he claimed for Spain.

Balboa suggested that the settlement be moved to the region of Darién, where the soil was more fertile and the Indians were thought to be friendlier. As the settlers approached that region, however, the local chieftain and about 500 men attacked the Spaniards. Despite the overwhelming numbers of the attackers, the Spanish defeated them after a fierce battle. The Indians fled into the rain forest, and the Spanish plundered gold and other valuables from their homes. In 1510, Balboa established the town of Santa Maria la Antigua del Darién in what is today Panama—the first permanent European settlement on the American mainland. Balboa eventually became mayor of Santa Maria and of the Spanish territory of Veragua, located along the eastern coast of Panama.

TO THE SOUTH SEA

In 1513, Balboa heard stories about "the other sea" from some of the local Indians. The tales told of a people to the south who were so wealthy that they ate from golden plates and drank from golden goblets. Balboa was warned, however, that these were a fierce people; a Spanish army of 1,000 men would be needed to defeat them. Balboa sought assistance from Hispaniola, but none came.

Balboa decided to lead an expedition to conquer "the other sea" and the wealthy Indians who lived near it. Balboa started his journey across the Isthmus of Panama on September 1, 1513. He was accompanied by about 190 Spanish soldiers and a few Indian guides. As Balboa and his men made their way through the dense forest, friendly Indians joined the expedition. As the force approached a mountain range near the Chucunaque River, the guides told Balboa that the other sea could be seen from the summit of the range. Balboa climbed the mountain, and on September 25, he saw the waters of the new—to the Europeans—sea. When he reached the shoreline two days later, he marched into the water and claimed the sea for Spain. Because he traveled southward across the isthmus to reach it, he named his discovery the South Sea.

Balboa and his men explored the area. They traded peacefully with some of the local peoples and defeated others in battle. As the Spaniards began to make their way back to Santa Maria, they accumulated treasure in the form of cotton goods, gold, and pearls. After they reached Santa Maria, Balboa dispatched a ship to tell the Spanish king the news of his discovery and give him his share of the treasure.

By 1518, Balboa had made many enemies. His rivals were jealous of his success and his wealth. Accused of **treason,** Balboa was arrested and sent back to Spain. There he was found guilty and sentenced to death for betraying his king. He was beheaded on January 15, 1519.

See also: Magellan, Ferdinand; New Spain; Pizarro, Francisco.

FURTHER READING

Marcovitz, Hal. *Vasco Nuñez De Balboa and the Discovery of the South Sea.* New York: Chelsea House, 2001.

Otfinoski, Steven. *Vasco Nunez De Balboa: Explorer of the Pacific.* New York: Benchmark Books, 2004.

Champlain, Samuel de (1567?–1635)

French explorer known as the father of New France, a French colony in North America. Samuel de Champlain was born into a Protestant family. The exact date of his birth is unknown. Some scholars believe that it was as early as 1567; others believe that it was as late as 1580. He learned sailing skills from his father or his uncle and soon became a respected navigator and cartographer.

EARLY EXPLORATIONS

In 1603, Champlain made his first voyage to what is today the eastern coast of Canada. He traveled up several of the rivers of the region and collected information about local geography. He used the information to make an accurate map of Canada from Hudson Bay in the north to the Great Lakes in the south. In 1604, Champlain made a second trip to the region. Impressed by Champlain's findings, the French king, Henry IV, asked the explorer to return to New France and locate a site for a permanent French settlement. Champlain spent three years exploring the area, from the Bay of Fundy southward to Cape Cod in what is today Massachusetts. He sailed home to France in 1607.

Champlain returned to New France in 1608 and founded a settlement that grew to become the city of Quebec. For protection, Champlain and his men built a fort two stories high surrounded by a moat. Twenty-eight settlers stayed to spend the winter at the new settlement, but only eight survived the harsh weather. The following summer, Champlain and his men worked to improve relations with the local Indians. He made **alliances** with the Huron, the Algonquin, and other groups in the region. The local Indians insisted that the French join them in an ongoing war with the Iroquois, who lived farther to the south. A small party of Frenchmen and Indians explored the Richelieu River and reached what is today Lake Champlain. On July 29, 1609, Champlain and his party encountered about 200 Iroquois. Fighting broke out, and Champlain shot and killed two Iroquois chiefs. The Iroquois fled but became lifelong enemies of the French.

LATER LIFE

In 1611, Champlain traveled to the area of what is today Montreal, where he continued to work for good relations with the Indians. He then retuned to France, where he sought support from the new French king, Louis XIII (r. 1610–1643). Louis gave Champlain the title of lieutenant, with authority to appoint officers, make treaties, and conduct wars with the local peoples.

Arriving back in New France in 1613, Champlain set out to the west in search of the **Northwest Passage,** a waterway that would be a shortcut to Asia. He spent the next three years exploring and trading with his Indian **allies.** In 1616, he set sail once again for France. He returned to New France in 1620 and spent the rest of his life there. Rather than continue exploring, however, he spent his time improving the administration of New France, working to build and fortify Quebec, and expanding the profitable fur trade with the Indians.

Champlain had a stroke in October 1535 and died on December 25 of that year. The site of his burial has been lost to history.

See also: France; Native Americans; *The Opening of the Fur Trade* in the "Viewpoints" section; Quebec.

FURTHER READING

Champlain, Samuel de. *The Voyages of Samuel de Champlain, Volume 1*. London: Echo Library, 2007.

Morganelli, Adriana. *Samuel de Champlain: From New France to Cape Cod*. New York: Crabtree Books, 2005.

Charters, Colonial

See Jamestown, Virginia; London Company; Plymouth Company.

Christianity

See Aztec Empire; Ferdinand and Isabella.

Colonialism and Disease

See Disease.

Colonies

See Plymouth Company; Thirteen Colonies; Roanoke, Lost Colony of.

Columbus, Christopher (1451–1506)

Italian explorer who, while sailing for Spain, crossed the Atlantic Ocean and sighted the lands that later were called the Americas. The Americas were colonized by a number of European countries.

Columbus was born in the Italian city of Genoa around 1451. His father was a weaver and merchant who traded in wine, cheese, and wool. Growing up close to the sea allowed young Columbus to learn basic seafaring skills. Later, Columbus signed up to work on a Genoese merchant ship. During a voyage in the eastern Atlantic, Columbus was shipwrecked on the coast of Portugal.

At the time, Portugal was one of the chief seafaring nations of western Europe. Under the guidance of Prince Henry the Navigator (1394–1460), Portugal became a leader in new methods of shipbuilding and ocean navigation. Columbus remained in Portugal and became a master mariner, learning to handle a newly developed type of ship known as the caravel. This new ship was faster and more maneuverable than older vessels. In time, Columbus made several voyages south along the African coast and traveled as far north as Iceland.

During these years in Portugal, Columbus developed his idea that became known as the Enterprise of the Indies. After studying both ancient and contemporary sources, Columbus became convinced that a ship could reach Cipango and Cathay—Japan and China—by sailing westward. Most educated Europeans of the time believed that the earth was round. Through careful observation, experienced sailors knew that the earth's surface was curved. The distance from Europe westward to Asia, however, was unknown.

Columbus thought that the distance between Europe and Asia was no more than 3,500 miles (5,600 kilometers). Some scholars of the time thought that the distance was greater. In reality, the distance from the Canary Islands, off the west coast of Africa—the place from which Columbus left Europe on his first voyage of discovery—to Japan is about 10,600 miles (16,900 kilometers).

In the early 1480s, Columbus proposed his idea of sailing west to Asia to Portugal's King John II (r. 1481–1495). The king was hesitant, however. In 1488, Bartholomeu Diaz returned from a voyage on which he successfully rounded the southern tip of Africa. Portugal then committed itself to finding a southern route to India and Asia. Rejected in Portugal, Columbus next turned to the rulers of Spain, King Ferdinand (r. 1479–1516) and Queen Isabella (r. 1474–1504). By 1492, the Spanish monarchs supported Columbus's idea and outfitted him with a crew of 90 men for the voyage.

A VOYAGE OF DISCOVERY

Christopher Columbus was an experienced sailor, and he took great care in his preparations for his trip across the Atlantic. He chose the Canary Islands—off the west coast of Africa—because of the northeasterly trade winds that blow around the islands. Columbus knew that sailors on the Atlantic had problems in more northern areas of the ocean because of the prevailing westerlies—winds that blow from the west. These winds made sailing westward difficult. Columbus also believed that his destination—Japan—was located at the same latitude as the Canaries.

Columbus's tiny fleet—the *Niña,* the *Pinta,* and the *Santa Maria*—sailed from Palos, Spain, in August 1492. The small ships stopped in the Canaries and took on more provisions. Then, on September 6, Columbus set out across the Atlantic. At first, the ships were helped by steady winds. As the winds became more variable

A–C

This painting by John Vanderlyn shows the Italian explorer Christopher Columbus's landing at the island of Guanahani in the West Indies, on October 12, 1492. His voyages westward across the Atlantic Ocean set the stage for later European colonization of the Americas.

and unpredictable, however, the trip grew longer, and the crew became worried and angry. By October 10, the crew of Columbus's flagship, the *Santa Maria*, was ready to **mutiny.** Columbus remained convinced that Asia lay just ahead.

Early on the morning of October 12, land—an island—was sighted. Going ashore, Columbus claimed the land for Spain and named the island San Salvador. Columbus, who most likely landed in the Bahamas, explored the island and traded with the local people. These people came to be called *Indians* because Columbus believed that he had reached the East Indies.

Columbus then continued on his journey, still searching for Japan or China. Sailing from San Salvador, he explored the northern coasts of what are today Cuba and Hispaniola—present-day Haiti and the Dominican Republic. In December, as he sailed along the coast of Hispaniola, the *Santa Maria* hit a reef and was destroyed. With two ships remaining, Columbus prepared to return to Spain. He took about 10 of the local people back with him. The ships arrived in Spain on March 15, 1493. Columbus was received with a triumphal welcome and given the title Admiral of the Ocean Sea.

LATER VOYAGES

On September 24, 1493, Columbus set sail from Cádiz, Spain, to find new territories and riches. This time his fleet included 17 ships and 1,200 men. Sailing from the Canary Islands on October 13, Columbus decided to follow a more southerly course. In early November, he sighted and named numerous small islands in the Caribbean Sea before again reaching Hispaniola and Cuba. Still believing that his party was very near China or Japan, he forced his men to swear a solemn oath that Cuba was a part of Asia. He found little gold or other riches, however, and returned to Spain in 1496.

Columbus set forth on a third voyage of discovery in 1498 with a fleet of six ships. He sent part of his fleet to Hispaniola to provide aid to the settlers he had left there on his second voyage. He led the other part of his fleet southward, toward the **equator,** in the hope of discovering more new lands. He ultimately discovered the island of Trinidad and sailed along the northern coast of South America. There, he discovered the Orinoco River, in what is today Venezuela. He then set sail for Hispaniola. On arriving there, however, he found the colonists fighting among themselves. Many of the colonists were angry because they had not found gold and other wealth. Others refused to work as hard as they needed to to make the new colony succeed.

It took Columbus two years to put down the revolt and restore order. Columbus agreed to give each of the colonists a tract of land and authority over the Indians who lived on it. Even after these measures, however, conditions on Hispaniola grew worse. After several months, Columbus requested that the Spanish monarchs send a judge to the island to deal with the situation. In response Ferdinand and Isabella sent Francisco de Bobadilla. Shortly after his arrival, Bobadilla seized Columbus and arrested him for mismanaging the colony. Columbus was placed in chains and returned to Spain. When he arrived in the city of Cádiz in November 1500, the king and queen immediately ordered Columbus's chains removed. Later, the royal court also restored all of Columbus's possessions but did not restore his titles. Columbus spent the next two years trying to recover his titles and clear himself of any wrongdoing.

In 1502, Columbus was able to convince Ferdinand and Isabella to fund a fourth voyage. To prevent any trouble on Hispaniola, they ordered Columbus not to land there. They charged him to search for the Straits of Malacca—an ocean passage in the East Indies—and to look for gold and other wealth. Columbus set sail in May 1502. He first landed at the Caribbean island of Martinique. Because a hurricane was approaching, Columbus then headed to Hispaniola, where he hoped to find a safe harbor. He arrived in Hispaniola on June 29 but was denied entrance to the port. He warned the new governor of the approaching hurricane, but the governor refused to listen. The governor ordered a fleet of 30 treasure ships to set sail for Spain. Columbus's ships took refuge in a small harbor and survived the hurricane with only minor damage. Only one of the ships of the treasure fleet survived the storm. Columbus sailed on to Jamaica and then to the coast of Central America, still in

History Speaks

Columbus's Log

Columbus's original ship's logs were lost in the 1500s, but several copies remain. The excerpts below are taken from a surviving copy of the log of his first voyage, in 1492.

Friday, 3 August 1492. Set sail from the bar of Saltes at 8 o'clock, and proceeded with a strong breeze till sunset, sixty miles or fifteen leagues south, afterwards southwest and south by west, which is the direction of the Canaries. . . .

Thursday, 9 August. The Admiral [Columbus] did not succeed in reaching the island of Gomera till Sunday night. Martin Alonzo remained at Grand Canary by command of the Admiral, he being unable to keep the other vessels company. The Admiral afterwards returned to Grand Canary, and there with much labor repaired the *Pinta,* being assisted by Martin Alonzo and the others; finally they sailed to Gomera. They saw a great eruption of flames from the Peak of Teneriffe, a lofty mountain. The *Pinta,* which before had carried latine sails, they altered and made her square-rigged. Returned to Gomera, Sunday, 2 September, with the *Pinta* repaired. . . .

Thursday, 11 October. Steered west-southwest; and encountered a heavier sea than they had met with before in the whole voyage. Saw. . . a green rush near the vessel. The crew of the *Pinta* saw a cane and a log; they also picked up a stick which appeared to have been carved with an iron tool, a piece of cane, a plant which grows on land, and a board. The crew of the *Niña* saw other signs of land, and a stalk loaded with rose berries. These signs encouraged them, and they all grew cheerful. Sailed this day till sunset, twenty-seven leagues.

Saturday, 13 October. At daybreak great multitudes of men came to the shore, all young and of fine shapes, very handsome; their hair not curled but straight and coarse like horse-hair, and all with foreheads and heads much broader than any people I had hitherto seen; their eyes were large and very beautiful; they were not black, but the color of the inhabitants of the Canaries, which is a very natural circumstance, they being in the same latitude with the island of Ferro in the Canaries. They were straight-limbed without exception, and not with prominent bellies but handsomely shaped. They came to the ship in canoes, made of a single trunk of a tree, wrought in a wonderful manner considering the country; some of them large enough to contain forty or forty-five men, others of different sizes down to those fitted to hold but a single person. . . .

search of Asia and gold. As they explored the Caribbean, Columbus's ships barely survived several huge storms. Columbus and his men arrived back in Spain on November 7, 1504. When Columbus died—in Valladolid, Spain, on May 20, 1506—he was 55 years old.

See also: New Spain; Vespucci, Amerigo.

FURTHER READING

Chrisp, Peter. *Christopher Columbus.* London: DK Press, 2006.

Doak, Robin S. *Christopher Columbus: Explorer of the New World.* Mankato, Minn.: Compass Point Press, 2005.

Cortés, Hernán (1485–1547)

See Aztec Empire.

D–F

Da Gama, Vasco (1460?–1524)

Portuguese explorer best known for leading an expedition around the southern tip of Africa to India. Vasco da Gama was born in the Portuguese town of Sines, on the southwestern coast. The exact year of his birth is debated; scholars believe that it was either 1460 or 1469.

Under the sponsorship of Prince Henry the Navigator (1394–1460), the Portuguese had been sailing south along the west coast of Africa since about 1420. In 1427, one of Henry's sailors discovered the islands of the Azores, to the west of Africa. By 1434, Portuguese ships had reached as far south as Cape Bojador, on the northwest African coast. Slowly, Portuguese navigators sailed along Africa's west coast, mapping the area and establishing small trading posts. By 1462, Portuguese sailors had reached the coast of what is today the country of Sierra Leone. Almost 25 years later, in 1488, Bartholomeu Diaz reached the southern tip of Africa, which he named the Cape of Storms. He quickly returned to Portugal with news of his voyage.

Recognizing that Dias's success opened an all-water route to Asia, Portugal's King John II (r. 1477–1495) renamed the tip of Africa the Cape of Good Hope.

FIRST VOYAGE TO INDIA

On July 8, 1497, Vasco da Gama left the Portuguese capital of Lisbon with four ships and a party of about 170 men. Da Gama's ships hugged the African coast until they reached the area of Sierra Leone. They then headed south into the open sea until, on December 16, they reached the point at which Dias had turned back. Da Gama sailed on, into the Indian Ocean, all the while keeping close to the eastern coast of Africa. He stopped and traded goods with the Islamic sultan of Mozambique and then sailed north to the coast of what is today Kenya. There he visited the African ports of Mombassa and Malindi. In one of those ports, da Gama hired an experienced sailor who knew that the **monsoon** winds would take the Portuguese ships directly to the west coast of India.

On May 20, 1498, da Gama's small fleet reached the Indian port of

Calicut. There, da Gama and his men at first found it difficult to establish trade with the local merchants but eventually had some success. Da Gama set sail to return to Portugal on August 29, 1498. Only two of his four ships made it home; they reached port in September 1499. King Manuel I (r. 1495–1521) welcomed da Gama with riches, named him a **hereditary** lord, gave him the title "Admiral of the Indian Sea," and made him the Earl of Vidigueria.

LATER VOYAGES

In 1502, da Gama set sail with 20 ships to enforce Portuguese interests in India and the east. On arriving in the Indian Ocean, he captured a Muslim ship that had sailed from Mecca, in what is today Saudi Arabia. He plundered the ship and locked all the passengers, who included several wealthy Muslim merchants, inside the hull. He then ordered the ship to be burned. Word of da Gama's astonishing cruelty spread, and when he reached the port of Calicut on October 30, the local ruler was eager to sign a trading treaty. Da Gama arrived back in Portugal in September 1503 and enjoyed the life of a noble.

Because of his fierce reputation, in 1524, Vasco da Gama was sent to India to replace the **viceroy,** or governor, of the Portuguese trading post. Da Gama contracted **malaria** and died in the city of Cochin on December 24, 1524. His body was buried in India but was moved to Portugal in 1539. In Portugal, he was reburied in a casket adorned with gold and jewels.

See also: Portugal.

FURTHER READING

Ames, Glenn J. *Vasco da Gama: Renaissance Crusader*. London: Longman, 2001.

Bailey, Katharine. *Vasco da Gama: Quest for the Spice Trade*. New York: Crabtree Books, 2007.

Koestler-Grack, Rachel A. *Vasco da Gama and the Sea Route to India*. New York: Chelsea House, 2005.

De Soto, Hernando (1496?–1542)

Spanish explorer who was the first European to explore what is today Florida and the southeastern United States and the first European to see the Mississippi River. De Soto was born some time between 1496 and 1500 in Extremadura, a poor region of the Spain. Little is known about his childhood, except that it was spent in two towns—Badajoz and Jerez de los Cabelleros.

Hernando de Soto sailed to the Americas in 1514 with the first governor of Darién, an area in what is today Panama. De Soto gained fame as an expert rider and fighter. He also became known for his cruelty toward Indians. In 1532, he joined the massive expedition of another Spanish explorer, Francisco Pizarro. Marching southward from Panama into what is today Peru, the Spaniards quickly conquered the wealthy Inca empire, which fell in 1533.

The Spaniards took untold wealth in gold and silver from the Incas. As one of the heros of the conquest, de Soto returned to Spain a rich man. He married Isabel de Bobadilla, a relative of the late Queen Isabella. Spain's King Charles V (r. 1516–1556) then appointed de Soto governor of Cuba and assigned him the task of colonizing the Americas.

RETURN TO THE AMERICAS

In early 1538, de Soto set sail from Spain and headed to Havana, the capital of Cuba. There, he established his rule as governor. In May 1539, he departed Havana and sailed northward to the western coast of Florida, which had been claimed and explored by the Spaniard Juan Ponce de León in 1513. De Soto sailed with more than 1,000 soldiers and sailors and nine ships—the largest expedition ever to explore the Americas.

The exact route of de Soto's expedition is not clear. He and his expedition probably stopped first at what is today Port Charlotte, Florida. He then traveled northward along the coast, stopping for the winter at the Indian village of Anhaica, near present-day Tallahassee, on the southern coast of the Florida **panhandle.** This is the only site at which **archeologists** have found firm evidence of de Soto's expedition.

After hearing stories of great amounts of gold to the northeast, de Soto and his men headed overland into what is today Georgia and South Carolina. Unsuccessful in the quest for riches, the group continued northward into present-day North Carolina, where de Soto rested for a month as he sent out small search parties to look for gold. The expedition then wandered westward, into what is today Tennessee and northern Georgia. From there, de Soto and his men moved south toward the Gulf of Mexico, where they planned to meet two ships from Havana that were bringing fresh supplies.

On the way southward, hostile Indians of the Mobilian people ambushed de Soto and his men. The Spaniards fought back but suffered serious casualties, including more than 20 dead and hundreds wounded. In addition, the Spaniards lost most of their supplies and horses. Fearful that the bad news would reach his supply ships, de Soto led the remains of his group westward into what is today Mississippi. There, the Spaniards spent the winter of 1540–1541.

In the spring of 1541, the group resumed its trek and continued westward. The Spaniards reached the Mississippi River on May 8, 1541. Hernando de Soto became the first European to see the mighty river. The river proved, however, to be a problem to cross. As they labored to build rafts on which to cross the Mississippi, the Spaniards were attacked repeatedly by unfriendly Indians. After spending about a month on the river's shore, the Spaniards finally crossed into what is today Arkansas. They eventually reached present-day Oklahoma and Texas as they continued on their search for gold. Returning eastward to the Arkansas River, the explorers endured a harsh winter encamped along its shore. By now, the men were exhausted. The explorers' interpreter died, and trading with the Indians for food and supplies became increasingly difficult.

In spring 1542, de Soto and his men returned to the Mississippi. In May, de Soto caught a fever and died. The men tried to conceal his death from the Indians, as de Soto had tried to convince them that Christians were **immortal.** They wrapped his body in blankets and weighted it with sandbags. Then, in the middle of the night, they sank the body in the middle of the Mississippi River.

The survivors of the expedition tried to return to the east but were

D–F

pushed back by hostile Indians. To escape, the Spaniards floated down the Mississippi River and into the Gulf of Mexico. On the gulf, the men stayed close to shore and eventually made their way to the small Spanish town of Pánuco, in Mexico, where they rested. The group then traveled to Mexico City, where they told their story to the Spanish governor.

Although de Soto's expedition failed to find any gold or establish any colonies, the survivors of the company provided Europeans with their first information about the geography and the peoples of what is today the North American southeast. In addition, some of the horses that escaped from de Soto's party formed the first herds of wild mustangs in North America.

See also: Inca Empire; Native Americans; New Spain; Spain.

FURTHER READING
Gallagher, Jim. *Hernando de Soto and the Exploration of Florida.* New York: Chelsea House, 2000.
Heinrichs, Ann. *De Soto: Hernando de Soto Explores the Southeast.* Mankato, Minn.: Compass Point Press, 2002.
Hubbard-Brown, Janet. *Hernando De Soto and His Expedition Across the Americas.* New York: Chelsea House, 2005.

Disease

Brought by European **colonists** to the Americas, various illnesses for which the native peoples had no natural defenses, thus causing widespread death among many tribes. In some instances, Europeans deliberately infected native Americans so that they would become sick and die. Most scholars believe that epidemic disease was the major cause of Native American population decline after the arrival of the Europeans.

EPIDEMIC DISEASE

Two common diseases that were prevalent, but not deadly, in Europe were chicken pox and measles. These two diseases were deadly to Native Americans. Smallpox, however, was the greatest killer of Native American populations. Epidemics often immediately followed European exploration and sometimes destroyed entire village populations. While precise figures are not available, some historians estimate that about 80 percent of some Native populations died due to European diseases after first coming into contact them.

In 1618 and 1619, smallpox wiped out 90 percent of the Massachusetts Bay Native Americans, who lived in what is today the New England area of the United States. Farther to the west, the Mohawk also were infected after contact with children of Dutch traders in the Albany, New York, area in 1634. The disease ravaged the native people. Smallpox swept through Mohawk villages, affecting groups living near Lake Ontario in 1636, and reaching the lands of the Iroquois by 1679, as it was carried by the Mohawk and other tribes who traveled the trading routes.

The native people living along the western coast of North America were not spared from similar epidemics. After first coming into contact with European explorers in the 1770s, smallpox rapidly killed at least 30 percent of the Native Americans who lived in what is today the northwest coast of the United States. For the next 80 to 100 years, smallpox and other diseases continued to devastate native populations in the region. By the mid-1800s, when large number of white settlers came to the area, the native population had decreased from about 37,000 to only 9,000.

AN ONGOING ISSUE

Smallpox epidemics continued to break out among native peoples. For example, in 1780-1782 and 1837-1838, smallpox epidemics brought devastation and a drastic decline in the population of the Plains Indians. By 1832, the federal government established a smallpox vaccination program for Native Americans, the first program created to address a health problem of American Indians.

See also: Native Americans.

Drake, Sir Francis (1540?–1595)

English explorer, slave trader, and politician. Francis Drake was born in Devon, England, probably about 1540. As with many of the famous **privateers** of this time, his exact date of his birth is unknown and little is known about his childhood.

In the late 1560s, Drake sailed with the first English slaving ships bringing enslaved Africans to the Americas. In the Gulf of Mexico, the Spanish attacked the English fleet and destroyed all but two of their ships. Drake escaped, but the incident made him regard the Spanish as his lifelong enemy.

TO THE PACIFIC

Drake set sail with five ships in December 1577. By October 1578, after a battle against the fierce storms at the Straits of Magellan, at the southern tip of South America, only one ship remained. Drake sailed that ship,

The Golden Hind, northward into the peaceful waters of the Pacific Ocean. As they made their way north along the western coast of South America, Drake and his men plundered Spanish ports and attacked Spanish ships, stealing huge amounts of treasure—gold, silver, and precious jewels.

By June 1579, still on its northward course, *The Golden Hind* had sailed past what is today San Diego, California. After Drake stopped to repair his ship and get supplies from friendly Indians he set sail again, still heading he north, in search of the fabled **Northwest Passage.**

Drake and his men reached as far north as what is today British Columbia, in Canada, and the **panhandle** of Alaska. Drake then turned his ship to the south and west. He sailed across the Pacific Ocean and reached the Moluccas, a group of islands in the East Indies, also known as the Spice Islands.

The Golden Hind then sailed westward, across the Indian Ocean and around the Cape of Good Hope, at the southern tip of Africa. Drake and his 59 remaining men reached the port of Plymouth, England, in September 1580. Thus, Drake became the first Englishman to **circumnavigate** the globe. On April 4, 1581, as a reward for Drake's successes, Queen Elizabeth I boarded *The Golden Hind* and had him knighted. The English saw Drake as a national hero, but the Spanish labeled him a pirate.

DEFEAT OF THE SPANISH ARMADA

In 1585, Drake sailed to the Americas and raided the Spanish ports of Santo Domingo and Cartagena, again stealing

D–F

gold, jewels, and other valuables. On his return voyage, he attacked the Spanish settlement at St. Augustine, in Florida. Furious at Drake's daring exploits, Philip II planned to invade England. Before war actually broke out, however, Drake boldly attacked Spain itself and destroyed more than 30 Spanish warships. By causing so much destruction, he delayed the planned invasion of England by at least a year.

In 1588, Spain assembled a fleet of 22 powerful **galleons** and more than 100 merchant ships that had been outfitted for battle. In May 1588, the huge fleet set sail, heading for the English Channel. Meanwhile, the English prepared for the attack. Lord Howard of Effingham was in charge, and Drake was second in command. The English fleet consisted of 34 warships and about 170 armed merchant ships.

The Spanish sailed up the English Channel in a crescent formation. When the Spanish reached the French port city of Calais, the English attacked. The smaller English ships were able to outmaneuver the huge Spanish galleons, and the English were better armed. Then, taking advantage of the flow of the tide and the cover of darkness, the English sent **fireships** among the Spanish fleet, causing the Spanish ships to scatter. The next morning, the two navies engaged in battle, and the English emerged victorious. The English fleet blocked the English Channel, however, thereby forcing the Spaniards to sail northward, around Scotland and Ireland, to return home. Along the way, the remains of the Spanish fleet encountered fierce storms that caused great damage. By the time the armada reached Spain, it had lost half of its ships and three-fourths of its men. England became the uncontested ruler of the seas.

See also: England; Magellan, Ferdinand; New Spain, Slavery and the Slave Trade; Spain.

FURTHER READING
Bawlf, Samuel. *The Secret Voyage of Sir Francis Drake, 1577–1580.* New York: Penguin, 2004.
Paige, Joy. *Sir Francis Drake: Circumnavigator of the Globe and Privateer for Queen Elizabeth.* New York: Rosen Publishing, 2002.

England

Nation located on the southern part of the island of Great Britain, situated across the English Channel northeast of the nation of France. England became a united nation sometime in the 900s. Its close connection to Europe was reinforced by the **Norman Conquest** of 1066. England's power grew, and by the late 1400s, the king was commissioning explorers to sail west in search of gold, spices, and the fabled **Northwest Passage.** In addition, English explorers looked for rich and fertile lands to colonize.

EARLY EXPLORATIONS
In 1496, King Henry VII (r. 1485–1509) hired an Italian explorer, John Cabot, to sail westward in an attempt to find the Norwest Passage and reach Asia. Cabot failed on his first voyage, reaching only as far as Iceland. The following year, Cabot set sail again. This time, he arrived at the eastern shore of what is today Canada, probably the coast of Newfoundland. Although he found no gold, he claimed the region for England. Henry VII was pleased with Cabot's successes, and

in 1498, he outfitted the explorer with five more ships. After setting sail from England, one of the ships stopped in Ireland for repairs. The remaining four ships, with John Cabot in command, sailed out to sea and were never heard from again.

John Cabot's son, Sebastian, was also a navigator and a mapmaker. Because Henry VII was still keen to find out more about the lands to the west, he funded a voyage to be led by Sebastian Cabot. The younger Cabot set sail in 1508 and was able to make detailed maps of the eastern coast of Canada. When the Cabot expedition returned to England, however, the men discovered that Henry VII had died and his son, Henry VIII (r. 1509–1547), had become king.

Henry VIII had little interest in overseas exploration. He devoted much of his foreign policy to European affairs. He tried especially to regain French lands that once had been ruled by English monarchs. Ultimately, Henry gained no land in France. He did, however, greatly expand his navy, thereby laying the foundation for England's rise as a powerful seafaring nation.

Henry VIII's young son, Edward VI (r. 1547–1553), assumed the throne in 1547. With the encouragement of his advisers, the young king authorized new voyages of discovery. One of the first trips was a trade expedition to Morocco, on the northern coast of Africa. Later voyages explored the western coast of Africa.

Once again in search of new routes to the riches of Asia, a fleet of three ships departed from London in 1553. Rather than sail westward, these ships, under the command of Hugh Willoughby, headed north and east, in the hope of finding a northeast passage to Asia. During a violent storm, the three ships were separated. Ultimately, Willoughby's ship became trapped in ice, and the entire crew froze to death. The other two ships, led by Richard Chancellor, fared better. They managed to reach the northern coast of Russia, and landed near the present-day city of Archangel. On hearing of the Englishmen's arrival, the czar, Ivan IV (r. 1533–1584), invited them to Moscow, the Russian capital. Successful negotiations led to the founding of the Muscovy Company, the first English **joint-stock company.** Soon, the Muscovy Company held a **monopoly** on trade between England and Russia.

A MAJOR EUROPEAN POWER

With the ascent of Elizabeth I (r. 1558–1603) to the English throne, England became a major European power and eventually ruled the seas. Among the most successful English explorers was Francis Drake. Drake first sailed as a **privateer.** Queen Elizabeth hired him to plunder the Spanish **colonies** on the western coast of the Americas. To get there, he crossed the Atlantic and traveled through the Straits of Magellan, at the southern tip of South America. Drake was able to **pillage** several Spanish ships and many colonial ports. He and his men carried off vast amounts of gold, silver, and other treasures. Drake then sailed northward along the coast of what is today the United States. He reached as far north as the Alaskan **panhandle.** From there, Drake sailed across the Pacific Ocean to the East Indies, where he traded with local

Under the rule of Queen Elizabeth I (r. 1588-1603), England became a world power and ruler of the seas. This engraving depicts the queen knighting the English adventurer Francis Drake on the deck of his ship, *The Golden Hind*. Drake's daring raids on Spanish colonies helped enrich England's treasury.

merchants for silks and spices. On his return to England in September 1580, the queen rewarded him with a knighthood, as well as a share of the **booty.**

In 1584, Walter Raleigh, another favorite of the queen, received a **charter** to explore and settle the eastern coast of North America. Raleigh sent an expedition to the Americas and named the land *Virginia* in honor of Elizabeth I, who was known as the Virgin Queen because she had never married. The group arrived on Roanoke Island, in what is today North Carolina, in August 1585 but returned to England the following year.

In 1587, Raleigh sent another expedition with more than 100 settlers —men, women, and children—to establish a permanent colony. Landing on Roanoke Island in July 1587, the settlers quickly built crude cabins and planted crops. In August 1587, the first English child was born in the Americas; her name was Virginia Dare. The following month, the expedition's leaders, including Virginia Dare's grandfather John White, returned to England for more supplies. Because of an ongoing war with Spain, however, White could not return to Roanoke until 1590. When he finally arrived, the settlers were gone. All that remained of the settlement were the letters CROATOAN carved on a tree. This caused some people to wonder whether the English settlers had moved to Croatoan Island or joined with the Croatoan Indians. Their true fate, however, remains a mystery.

SUCCESS

In 1607, about 100 men and boys landed in Virginia and established the settlement of Jamestown, named for King James I (r. 1603–1625). Harsh conditions, disease, famine, and attacks by Indians threatened the colony's survival. Fortunately, more colonists, including women and children, and fresh supplies arrived in June 1610. In 1612, one of the colonists, John Rolfe, began to grow tobacco, which was becoming popular in Europe. Soon, the Virginia colony was **exporting** tons of tobacco to Europe.

The success of the Virginia colony led others in England to establish colonies in the Americas. By 1733, England had founded a total of thirteen colonies along the Atlantic Seaboard.

See also: Drake, Sir Francis; Jamestown, Virginia; New England; Spain; Plymouth Company; Roanoke, Lost Colony of; Thirteen Colonies; Tobacco.

FURTHER READING

Aronson, Marc. *Sir Walter Raleigh and the Quest for El Dorado.* Boston: Clarion Books, 2000.

Bawlf, Samuel. *The Secret Voyage of Sir Francis Drake, 1577–1580.* New York: Penguin, 2004.

Kelso, William M. *Jamestown: The Buried Truth.* Charlottesville: University of Virginia Press, 2006.

Miller, Jake. *The Lost Colony of Roanoke.* New York: PowerKids Press, 2005.

Paige, Joy. *Sir Francis Drake: Circumnavigator of the Globe and Privateer for Queen Elizabeth.* New York: Rosen Publishing, 2002.

Ferdinand (1452–1516) and Isabella (1451–1504)

Monarchs, or rulers, who unified Spain and set the stage for Spanish exploration and colonization, or settlement, of the Americas. The marriage of these royal cousins, Ferdinand of Aragon and Isabella of Castille, helped establish Spain as a major European power. In 1492, their joint forces drove the Muslims from Granada, the last Islamic kingdom on the **Iberian Peninsula.**

Devoutly Catholic, the monarchs attempted to ensure that all Spaniards followed the teachings of the Roman Catholic Church. In 1492, Ferdinand and Isabella began to persecute the Jews. The rulers tried to force all Jews living in Spain either to leave the country or to convert to Catholicism. About 200,000 Jews chose to leave rather than convert.

FIRST VOYAGES OF DISCOVERY

In 1486, the Italian explorer Christopher Columbus met with Ferdinand and Isabella to present his plan to sail westward in search of Asia. The monarchs consulted with their advisers, who recommended against financing Columbus's idea. Undiscouraged, Columbus continued to try to persuade the monarchs to support his plan. Finally, in 1492, the monarchs agreed to give Columbus three ships and a crew of about 90 men. Columbus was to seek a westward route to Asia, search for gold and other riches, and convert the native people to Christianity.

Columbus's fleet set sail from Palos, Spain, in August 1492 and landed in

D–F

the Americas on October 12. His ships sailed along the northern coasts of the two islands that are today Cuba and Hispaniola (Haiti and the Dominican Republic). Believing that he had reached India, he called the people he found "Indians." Columbus found little treasure, but he claimed the land for Spain. He returned home with exotic plants and animals. About 10 Indians also traveled with Columbus and his men. Columbus was convinced that he had reached islands near the coast of Asia. He persuaded Ferdinand and Isabella to fund three more voyages of discovery.

LEGACY

Because of Columbus's voyages, Ferdinand and Isabella sent other explorers, **conquistadors,** and **missionaries** to the Americas. Like Columbus before them, these Spaniards were told to search for an all-water route to Asia; look for spices, gold, and other riches; and convert the local people to Christianity.

Isabella died in 1504, but Ferdinand continued the crown's support for exploration. By the time of Ferdinand's death in 1516, Spanish conquistadors had explored most of the islands in the Caribbean Sea and established colonies there. The Spanish explored the coast of Florida and the eastern coasts of Mexico and Central America, as well as northern South America. In 1513, the conquistador Vasco Nuñez de Balboa crossed the **Isthmus** of Panama and became the first European to see the Pacific Ocean. Naming his find the South Sea, Balboa claimed it for the Spanish crown.

See also: Balboa, Vasco Nuñez de; Columbus, Christopher; New Spain; Spain; Vespucci, Amerigo.

FURTHER READING
Edwards, J. *Ferdinand and Isabella: Profiles in Power*. Upper Saddle River, N.J.: Longman, 2004.
Whitelaw, Nancy. *Queen Isabella: And the Unification of Spain*. Greensboro: N.C.: Morgan Reynolds, 2004.

France

Nation in Western Europe and one the leading countries during the Age of Exploration, from the early fifteenth to the early seventeenth centuries. Because of ongoing wars in Europe, France did not turn to overseas exploration until after 1500. By that time, France was a major European power and began vying with rivals England and Spain for overseas land and wealth.

FIRST VOYAGES

King Francis I (r. 1515–1547) first hired the Italian explorer Giovanni da Verrazano to sail westward in search of the **Northwest Passage.** Verrazano set sail in 1524 and reached the coast of what are today the Carolinas. He then sailed northward, becoming the first European to explore the eastern coast of North America. He continued to search for a route to Asia and eventually reached what is known today as the Narrows in lower New York Harbor. From New York Harbor, he sailed along the southern coast of Long Island and reached Narragansett Bay in what is today Rhode Island. There, he probably met the Narragansett people. Verrazano proceeded around Cape Cod and then hugged the coasts of

Maine and Nova Scotia until, eventually, he reached Newfoundland. He claimed Newfoundland for France and then set sail for home, across the Atlantic.

In 1534, Francis I sent Jacques Cartier to continue his nation's voyages of discovery, to search for gold and other riches, and to continue to look for the fabled Northwest Passage. On May 10 of that year, Cartier arrived in Newfoundland but was disappointed by the barren landscape. He sailed to the southwest and reached the fertile island now called Prince Edward Island. From there he sailed on and became the first European to see the Gulf of St. Lawrence, which he claimed for France.

The following year, on a second voyage of discovery, Cartier again reached the St. Lawrence. This time, he traveled up the river as far as present-day Montreal, where he traded with the local Indians. As winter approached, he sailed down the river to the site of the present-day city of Quebec. There, Cartier and his men set up camp. They returned to France the following spring. Cartier made one more trip to the St. Lawrence region, in 1541–1542. Again, he explored the region in search of gold or other riches. Cartier never attempted to establish a permanent settlement in the Americas.

In 1542, the French explorer Jean-François de La Rocque de Roberval established a settlement at Charlesbourg-Royal, in present-day Quebec, where Cartier had earlier built a fort. This first attempt at colonization failed because of the brutal winter and hostile Indians. The colonists returned to France the following year.

LATER SUCCESSES

In the early 1600s, Samuel de Champlain made several voyages to what is today Canada. He established the first permanent settlement, Quebec, in 1608. The settlement grew slowly, and by 1663, about 550 people lived in the town itself and about 1,400 lived in the surrounding countryside.

By the 1630s, French explorers had moved farther inland. In 1633, Jean Nicolet became the first European to see Lake Michigan. He then pushed farther west and reached what is today the state of Wisconsin, near Green Bay. On learning that the local people were called the Winnebago, meaning "People of the Sea," Nicolet was certain that he was near the Pacific Ocean and close to finding a route to Asia.

Marquette and Joliet By the 1670s, French explorers and **missionaries** had moved deep into North America. In 1673, explorer Louis Joliet and Jesuit priest Jacques Marquette canoed across Lake Michigan and then portaged (carried their boats and supplies overland) to what is today the Wisconsin River. Joliet and Marquette eventually reached the Mississippi River. They were the first Europeans to see the Mississippi. The men sailed southward on the river as far as what is today Arkansas and then returned north.

La Salle In 1682, Robert de La Salle canoed south on the Mississippi River and reached its mouth on the Gulf of Mexico. La Salle claimed all the land drained by the Mississippi for France and named the area Louisiana in honor of the French king, Louis XIV (r. 1638–1715). In 1684, La Salle set

D–F

sail from France with four ships and 300 colonists. He planned to establish a colony at the mouth of the Mississippi. Unfortunately, the small fleet was plagued by misfortune. One ship was lost to pirates in the West Indies, a second ship sank, and a third ran aground near what is today Matagorda Bay, Texas. The survivors established a settlement called Fort St. Louis, near what is today Inez, Texas. The colonists then tried three times, unsuccessfully, to make their way east to the Mississippi. On a fourth attempt, the 36 survivors mutinied. La Salle was murdered by mutineers on March 19, 1687. The colony at Fort St. Louis lasted until 1688, when hostile Indians killed the 20 remaining adults and took five children captive.

La Salle's plan was finally fulfilled in 1718, when Jean-Baptiste Le Moyne, Sieur de Bienville, founded New Orleans near the mouth of the Mississippi. He carefully chose the site—a bend in the Mississippi—because it would allow the French to control river traffic. Thus situated, the French could tax goods headed to or from the nearby Gulf of Mexico. The strategic location also enabled the French to prevent rivals Britain and Spain from using the river to further their settlement of America.

Throughout the first half of the 1700s, the French built a string of forts, starting in Canada and extending down to the Gulf of Mexico. The forts served as trading posts for dealings with the Indians, as the French had established a highly profitable fur trade. By the 1750s, however, French traders and English settlers were coming into conflict.

See also: Champlain, Samuel de; French and Indian War; Marquette, Jacques and Louis Joliet; New France, Quebec.

FURTHER READING

Chartrand, Rene. *The Forts of New France in Northeast America, 1600–1763.* Oxford: Osprey, 2008.

Parkman, Francis. *La Salle and the Discovery of the Great West.* New York: Modern Library, 1999.

Worth, Richard. *Voices from Colonial America: New France, 1534–1763.* Washington, D.C.: National Geographic Children's Press, 2007.

French and Indian War (1754–1763)

Name given to the fighting in North America between Great Britain and France during a worldwide conflict known as the Seven Years' War. The conflict in North America received its name because the British **colonists** were fighting the French and their Indian **allies.** As a result of the war, France lost most of its holdings in North America, and Great Britain became the major power on the continent.

BEGINNINGS OF THE CONFLICT

From the late 1690s, both the British and the French claimed the lands around Nova Scotia, Lake Champlain, the Great Lakes, and the Ohio River Valley. Between 1689 and 1748, the two European powers fought a series of three wars in Europe and in North America. None of these conflicts—King William's War (1689–1697), Queen Anne's War (1702–1713), and King George's War (1744–1748)—completely resolved the question of ownership of these vast lands.

By the 1750s, the Ohio Valley had become the main point of conflict between the two powers. The French wanted the area because it provided the shortest route between French settlements in Canada and in the Mississippi River Valley. The British wanted the land so that their American colonies eventually could expand westward. Both nations wanted the region for the profitable fur trade.

To strengthen French claims, the governor of Canada sent expeditions into the area beginning in 1749. In addition, in 1752, the French built a string of forts in the eastern part of the valley.

At the same time, the British also worked to strengthen their claims to the region. A colonial land-**speculating** company, the Ohio Company, wanted to increase trade with the Indians and build forts and settlements in the Ohio Valley. It was hoped that this activity would encourage colonists to settle the area and buy land from the company. To further its claim, the British government sent word to all its colonial governors that any intrusion by a foreign power on land claimed by the British was to be stopped, by force if necessary.

In 1753, Governor Robert Dinwiddie of Virginia sent George Washington, to warn the French they were on British land. The French responded that they were on their own land and that they would not leave. Washington reported the French reply to Dinwiddie, who then sent Captain William Trent to build a fort in the disputed region, at the point where the Allegheny and Monongahela rivers join to form the Ohio River. The French, however, drove Trent away and built their own fort—Fort Duquesne.

In May 1754, a clash occurred between the French and colonial forces under Washington at Great Meadows, to the south of Fort Duquesne. After defeating the French, Washington ordered that a fort be built at Great Meadows—Fort Necessity. A small French force laid siege to the fort and forced Washington to surrender in July 1754. Thus began the Seven Years' War.

Meeting with the Iroquois Even before the British were forced to flee from the Ohio Valley, several of their colonial leaders were trying to find a way to meet the French and Indian threat. In June 1754, delegates from seven colonies met with about 150 Iroquois leaders in Albany, New York.

The British colonial leaders tried to persuade the Iroquois, who were bitter enemies of the French, to join in an alliance with the British colonists against the French and their Indian allies. The Iroquois, however, left the meeting without making any promises to the British.

The Albany Plan of Union At the same time that the meeting with the Iroquois was taking place, other British colonial leaders were discussing plans to unite the colonies. After some debate, these leaders endorsed a plan based on the ideas of Benjamin Franklin.

According to this plan—the Albany Plan of Union—a colonial chief executive, to be known as the president general, was to be appointed by the **British crown.** A council was to be chosen by the colonial assemblies. The council was given the power to control relations with the Indians, raise and equip a colonial army, build forts, and levy taxes to carry out these activities.

When the plan was sent to the colonial assemblies, the assemblies did not like it. They felt that they would lose too much power and that the plan would lead to higher taxes and to additional British interference in American affairs.

FIGHTING THE WAR

In April 1755, the British sent General Edward Braddock to the colonies to assume command of the British forces and defeat the French. Braddock's first objective was to capture Fort Duquesne and drive the French from the Ohio Valley. With about 1,400 British soldiers and another 450 members of the colonial **militia** under George Washington, Braddock began his campaign. After moving to within about eight miles (12.8 kilometers) of the fort, the British forces were ambushed by the French and their Indian allies. The British retreated.

At first, French victories mounted. In 1756, the French captured Fort Oswego, and in 1757, they took control of Fort William Henry, both on the New York frontier. In spring 1757, however, British war policies changed after William Pitt became prime minister and the leader of the House of Commons in the British Parliament.

Pitt took complete control of the war effort. He called for an offensive war against the French. He reorganized the British army and navy and replaced older officers with younger leaders. He also urged the colonists to take a more active role in their defense by enlisting more colonial soldiers. With Pitt's leadership, the direction of the war turned in favor of the British.

In 1758, British forces captured the French forts at Louisbourg, Frontenac, and Duquesne. In 1759, British general James Wolfe captured Quebec. Montreal, the last important French stronghold in North America, fell in 1760. These victories in America, as well as military successes in other parts of the world, led the French to seek truce talks in 1762.

THE TREATY OF PARIS

The French and Indian War ended with a humiliating defeat for France. After the completion of peace talks, Great Britain, France, and Spain signed a final agreement, known as the Treaty of Paris of 1763. Spain became involved in these talks because the British had declared war on Spain in 1762 and had seized several Spanish possessions.

Under the terms of this treaty, Great Britain gained all of Canada and all French land east of the Mississippi River, as well as all French holdings in India. France was allowed to keep two islands at the mouth of the St. Lawrence River. For siding with France during the war, Spain lost Florida to Great Britain, but Britain returned Cuba and the Philippines to Spanish rule. To compensate Spain for the loss of Florida, France **ceded** its land west of the Mississippi, the vast tract known as Louisiana, to Spain.

With the signing of the Treaty of Paris, French power in North American came to an end. At the same time, Great Britain acquired a worldwide empire.

See also: New England; New France; Proclamation of 1763; Quebec.

FURTHER READING

Anderson, Fred. *The War That Made America: A Short History of the French and Indian War.* New York: Penguin, 2006.

Borneman, Walter R. *The French and Indian War: Deciding the Fate of America.* New York: Harper Perennial, 2007.

H–L

Hudson, Henry (1570?–1611)

English explorer who discovered what is today the Hudson River in New York and Hudson Bay in Canada. Little is known about Henry Hudson's early life. He probably signed on as a cabin boy and eventually worked his way up to ship's captain.

In 1607, the Muscovy Company of England hired Hudson to search for a Northeast Passage to Asia. Hudson sailed northward from England and reached islands off the northern coast of Norway. On a second voyage, in 1608, he discovered some islands off the northern coast of Russia in the Arctic Ocean. Both times, after encountering ice and harsh conditions, he returned home to England without success.

HUDSON RIVER

In 1609, the Dutch East India Company hired Henry Hudson to sail west and search for the **Northwest Passage.** With a crew of 20 on his ship, the *Half Moon*, Hudson sailed southwest and reached what is today the coast of Maine. After trading with the local Indians, he and his crew sailed southward along the coast. They reached as far south as what is today the Chesapeake Bay in Maryland. Realizing that this was not the Northwest Passage, Hudson turned north and reached the mouth of the Hudson River. Hudson claimed the area for the Dutch. Later, the Dutch colony of New Netherland was established in the region. Believing that he might have discovered the sought-after passage to Asia, Hudson began to explore the river on September 12, 1609.

Hudson sailed as far north as the present-day city of Albany, New York, where the river narrows and becomes shallow. Disappointed, he turned around after two days and sailed downriver to the island of Manhattan. On October 4, the *Half Moon* set sail for home. Hudson reached Devonshire, England, on November 7. He and his crew were not permitted to leave England, and the ship eventually returned to the Netherlands without them.

HUDSON BAY

In 1610, Hudson set off on his final journey. A group of wealthy London business leaders hired Hudson to search once again for the Northwest Passage. Setting sail on the *Discovery,* Hudson traveled north. He reached the coast of Iceland and then continued west. He reached a **strait,** now know as Hudson Strait, located at the northern tip of Labrador, and then entered what is today Hudson Bay. The *Discovery* became trapped in the ice

In 1609, Henry Hudson sailed into what is today the Hudson River, on the *Half Moon*. The discovery is depicted in this painting by Albert Bienstadt (1830–1902).

and was forced to spend the winter there. In spring 1611, Hudson wanted to continue his explorations, but his crew, who wished to return home, **mutinied.** Hudson, his teenage son John, and seven or eight loyal crewmembers were set adrift in the bay. They were never seen again.

Only eight of the crew aboard the *Discovery* made it back to England. Although they were arrested, they were never punished for Hudson's death. Because of Hudson's explorations, however, England claimed the land around the bay and established a profitable fur trade with the Indians who lived in the area.

See also: England; Netherlands; New Netherland.

FURTHER READING

Gleason, Carrie. *Henry Hudson: Seeking the Northwest Passage.* New York: Crabtree, 2005.

Sandler, Corey. *Henry Hudson: Dreams and Obsession: The Tragic Legacy of the New World's Least Understood Explorer.* New York: Citadel, 2007.

Inca Empire

In South America, a great Native American civilization that reached its peak in the early 1500s and was conquered by Spanish **conquistadors** in 1533. By the late 1400s, the Inca ruled over a vast empire that included parts of what are today Columbia, Ecuador, Peru, Bolivia, Chile, and Argentina.

The empire extended more than 2,500 miles (4,000 kilometers) along the Pacific coast of South America. From their capital, the centrally located city of Cuzco, the Inca ruled over many diverse peoples.

GOVERNMENT

Inca government was highly ordered and was very efficient. It was organized on an ancient division of Inca society called the ayllu, or clan. Local representatives of the central government supervised groups of ayllus, which in turn made up increasingly larger organized groups that were responsible to the central government in Cuzco. At the top of the government was the absolute ruler—the Inca—who was worshipped as a god by those he ruled.

SOCIETY

The Inca were primarily farmers. Because of the rugged terrain of the Andean Highlands where they lived, Inca farmers built **terraced fields** and used widespread **irrigation.** All lands belonged to the Inca but were used in common by the allyus. The Inca was responsible for the well-being of his people. For example, **surplus** crops were collected by the government and were used for trade or held for times of **famine.**

Inca society was headed by the royal family and a class of nobles. Because the empire was so vast, administrative officials made up an important upper class of people in Inca society. Tradespeople, such as artisans and merchants, made up another social class. The common people, the peasants and laborers, made up the lowest and largest social class.

The common people of the empire were required to set aside a time every year during which they worked only for the Inca. Very few people were exempt from this annual labor. During this time, artisans, for example, made weapons for the army and ornaments for religious purposes. Other people paved roads or worked on building the great palaces and stone temples found across the empire. Some men served as soldiers or as chasquis, runners who carried messages and packages throughout the empire.

ACHIEVEMENTS

The Inca civilization is noted for several important achievements. The Inca used a lunar calendar and developed a complex system of mathematics that included the use of the decimal point and the concept of zero. The Inca did not, however, develop a system of writing. The Inca used medicines, such as quinine, that are still in use today. Mining operations and advanced **smelting,** or ore refining methods, provided rich stores of gold and silver for the Inca.

The Inca built roads and suspension bridges to link their far-flung empire. These roads were not for the use of the common people, however. Only the chasquis, the army, and government officials were allowed to use them. The common people were not allowed to travel outside of their local villages.

The Inca empire reached its height of power and influence in the early 1500s. At that time, the ruling Inca divided the empire between his two sons. The two sons then fought to take complete control of the empire. In 1532, one of the sons, Atahualpa, finally dominated the entire empire. It was the same year that the Europeans first entered Inca lands.

CONQUEST OF THE INCA

In 1532, the Spanish conquistador Francisco Pizarro sailed southward from Panama with a small army of about 180 men, 27 horses, and two cannons. He was searching for the Inca empire, as he had heard stories of the Inca's great wealth of gold and silver. The tiny Spanish force invaded the huge, well-organized empire, with its population of more than 6 million people. Timing, however, was in favor of the Spaniards. The empire had been weakened by the recently ended civil war between the two sons of the last ruler. In addition, the Inca knew nothing about horses or firearms, thus giving the Spaniards another advantage.

Pizarro marched for almost two months toward the town of Cajamarca, where Atahualpa was resting after having defeated his brother. Pizarro sent messengers to arrange a meeting. Atahualpa, however, refused to meet with the Spaniards. This refusal led Pizarro to attack the Inca army on November 16, 1532. With their superior weapons, the Spaniards easily defeated the Inca army and executed Atahualpa's personal guards. Pizarro then took Atahualpa captive.

To win his release, Atahualpa promised to fill one room that measured 22 feet (7 meters) by 17 feet (5 meters) with gold and two rooms of the same size with silver. After receiving the ransom, however, Pizarro had Atahualpa executed by garrote, or strangulation, on the false charge that he had murdered his brother. Leaderless and disorganized, the Inca were not able to resist the Spanish advance into their lands. Cuzco, the capital, fell in 1533, and Pizarro claimed the land for Spain. Pizarro then founded Lima as the new capital of Peru. Ultimately, greed and jealousy among the Spaniards led to the murder of Pizarro in 1541.

See also: Aztec Empire; Balboa, Vasco Nuñez de; *The Diversity of Native America* in the "Viewpoints" section; Spain.

FURTHER READING

DiConsiglio, John. *Francisco Pizarro: Destroyer of the Inca Empire.* New York: Franklin Watts, 2008.

MacQuarrie, Kim. *The Last Days of the Incas.* New York: Simon & Schuster, 2007.

Somerville, Barbara A. *Empire of the Inca.* New York: Facts On File, 2004.

Indentured Servitude

See Jamestown, Virginia; London Company.

Jamestown, Virginia

First permanent English settlement in the Americas. In 1606, the new king of England, James I (r. 1603–1625), granted a group of English merchants a **charter** to establish the Virginia Company. This **joint-stock company** was charged with settling Virginia and turning the colony into a profitable business as well as with finding gold and an all-water route to Asia. In May 1607, about 100 men and boys arrived in Virginia and established the settlement of Jamestown, named in honor of King James I.

The settlers built a triangular-shaped fort around a storehouse, a church, and several cabins. Disease, **famine,** and attacks from Indians threatened the settlement's survival, however. The stern British captain John Smith probably saved the colony by enforcing strict rules. Among these were, "He who does not work, does not eat." In October 1609, Smith was injured in a gunpowder accident and returned to England for treatment. He never returned to Virginia.

Without firm leadership, the survival of the colony again became threatened. **Colonists** grew lazy. Rather than plant crops or hunt in the forest, they foolishly searched for gold and other riches. Food became so scarce that the winter of 1609–1610 has become known as the "starving time," and more than half of the colonists died. In June 1610, the remaining colonists decided to return to England. As they sailed down the James River, they met a fleet of ships bringing supplies and more settlers from England. The settlers returned to their fort, and the colony slowly began to thrive.

PROSPERITY AND PEACE

One of the key reasons that Jamestown began to prosper was the planting of tobacco. In 1612, one of the colonists, John Rolfe, began to grow a mild tobacco plant. Tobacco had been introduced to Europe from Spain's American colonies and had become very popular. By 1619, Jamestown had **exported** 10 tons of tobacco to Europe, making the colony financially successful. The colonists were able to trade their tobacco for other goods.

In 1614, John Rolfe married Pocahontas, the daughter of Powhatan, an Algonquin chief. After this marriage, relations between the settlers and the Indians grew more peaceful.

Jamestown became the first successful English settlement in the Americas. As Jamestown prospered, more colonists arrived from England and the settlement grew into the colony of Virginia. By 1733, England had established 12 more colonies along the Atlantic Seaboard.

GOVERNMENT

By 1619, the Virginia colony had grown significantly. Governor George Yeardley arrived in the colony in the spring of that year and recommended that each settlement send two representatives, or burgesses, to Jamestown to represent the people. That summer, the **House of Burgesses,** the first representative assembly in the Americas, met in a church in Jamestown. The burgesses passed several laws and approved the so-called "great charter" that became the first constitution for the colony of Virginia.

FIRST AFRICAN SLAVES

In August 1619, a Dutch slave-trading ship stopped at Jamestown. Onboard were about 20 Africans; the ship's captain traded these people to the Jamestown colonists for food. These first Africans were not slaves, but **indentured servants,** who, like many poor Englishmen, traded seven years of labor for the cost of passage to the Americas. These African American indentured servants worked in the tobacco fields. After their period of

Settled in 1607, Jamestown, Virginia, was the first permanent English colony in North America. Even today, archeologists and historians are discovering more information about this historic site.

indenture was fulfilled, they were freed from their contracts.

See also: England; Native Americans; New England; Slavery and the Slave Trade; Thirteen Colonies; Tobacco.

FURTHER READING

Kelso, William M. *Jamestown: The Buried Truth.* Charlottesville: University of Virginia Press, 2006.

Kupperman, Karen Ordahl. *The Jamestown Project.* Cambridge, Mass.: Belknap Press, 2007.

Sakurai, Gail. *The Jamestown Colony.* New York: Children's' Press, 1997.

King Philip's War

See New England.

London Company

An English company established by royal **charter** by King James I (r. 1603–1625) of England on April 10, 1606. The company's purpose was to establish profitable settlements in North America. Not originally founded as a **joint-stock company,** the London Company became one under a revised 1609 charter.

The lands granted to the London Company included the eastern coast of North America from the 34th parallel (near present-day Cape Fear in North Carolina) northward to the 41st parallel (in Long Island Sound). On May 14, 1607, the London Company established Jamestown, Virginia, on the James River about 40 miles (64 kilometers) upstream from the mouth of the Chesapeake Bay. Jamestown became the first permanent English settlement in the present-day United States. The company also accidentally settled The Somers Isles (present-day Bermuda) colony in 1609, while sending additional supplies to Jamestown.

The company's business was to settle the Virginia colony using voluntary workers under the **indentured servant** system. Under this system, the company provided passage, food, protection, and eventual land ownership to indentured workers, who could not afford to pay the costs themselves, in exchange for seven years of labor for the company.

In addition to settling the new colony, the early Jamestown **colonists** had another important mission. They were to make a profit for the owners of the company. The settlers could not devote as much time to their profit-making responsibilities as the company wanted, however. They were too busy simply trying to stay alive.

Unfortunately for the Jamestown settlers, a ship carrying supplies for the colony was shipwrecked in Bermuda in July 1609. When Sir Thomas Gates and the other survivors of the shipwreck finally arrived in Jamestown in 1610, they found only 60 of the original colonists alive. The others had perished during the "starving time," the harsh winter of 1609–1610. Most of the remaining colonists were ill or dying.

FAILURE AT JAMESTOWN

Despite the abundance of food that Gates and the other shipwreck survivors had brought from Bermuda, the Jamestown colony did not have the means for survival. It was decided to return to England. The Jamestown survivors went aboard Gates's ship, and the colony was to be abandoned. Just as the ship was departing, another relief fleet carrying more colonists and supplies arrived. All the settlers went ashore again, and the Jamestown colony tried to begin again.

As news of the Jamestown colony's woeful state reached England, the London Company was hit with financial catastrophe. Because of the London Company's poor economic condition, many stockholders of the company refused to pay for their shares. The company then became involved in dozens of court cases as it tried to collect the money it was owed. On top of these losses, the company went further into debt when it sent hundreds of additional colonists to Virginia in the early 1610s.

The company could do little to get out from under its crushing debt. No gold had been found in Virginia. Attempts to produce glass, pitch, and tar at Jamestown had been barely profitable. It was more cost effective to produce such items in Europe.

Faced with bad publicity, fighting among the **stockholders,** and ongoing financial woes, the company—by now called the Virginia Company—organized a great advertising campaign in the early 1600s. The company papered London street corners with tempting **broadsheets** and published enticing newspaper articles. The company even convinced the clergy to preach about the importance of supporting colonization. Before the company went **bankrupt,** it published

Then & Now

Business Organizations

In precolonial times, **sole proprietorships** and **partnerships** were the most common forms of business organizations. The **joint-stock company,** however, was a corporation in which a group of people organized their business under a charter granted by a government. Many of the English colonies were established by such companies.

A company enjoyed many of the rights of an individual. For example, it could hold property, contract debts, hire workers, and sue in court. It also could acquire large amounts of capital, or money, by selling stock, or ownership, to investors. People who bought shares of stock—stockholders—owned the corporation. They were entitled to vote at stockholders' meetings, and the owners of a majority of the stock could control the corporation.

In the early years of the United States, few businesses were organized as corpora-tions. After the Civil War (1861–1865), how-ever, the corporation became a powerful force in the nation's economy. By the late 1800s, corporations produced two-thirds of the nation's industrial output.

Importantly, corporations with large amounts of capital could more easily de-velop the transportation and communi-cation systems that the nation needed at that time. In addition, corporations could supply increasing quantities of the raw materials necessary to feed the nation's ever-growing number of factories.

Today, corporations make up the vast majority of businesses in the United States. Corporations make possible the widespread ownership of businesses and industries. People who do not have enough money to establish their own businesses can buy shares of a stock in companies that they believe will be profitable.

27 pamphlets and books promoting the Virginia colony.

As it tried to drum up support for its endeavors, the Virginia Company also changed its sales approach. Rather than promise vast profits to investors, the company decided to play to patriotic sentiment and na-tional pride. Potential stockholders were told that the purchase of shares would help build the might of Eng-land and make the nation the power it deserved to be. They also were told that the "heathen natives" would be converted to the "proper form of Christianity," the Church of England.

People who were out of work were told that they could find employment in the Americas. Thus, the public was informed, the standard of living would increase throughout England.

The English took the advertising to heart. The upper classes wished to prove their loyalty to the crown. Mem-bers of the growing **middle class** saw stock purchases not only as pa-triotic, but also as a way to improve themselves financially. The population of Jamestown rose, but a high death rate among the settlers kept profits unstable. The company's debts kept increasing.

SUCCESS WITH TOBACCO

The colony remained unstable and unprofitable until John Rolfe's success with tobacco as a **cash crop.** The tobacco originally grown in Virginia did not appeal to either the English settlers or the market in England. A different, sweeter type of tobacco that was grown in the Caribbean region was favored. In 1611, Rolfe brought the hard-to-obtain Caribbean tobacco seeds back to Jamestown from the island of Trinidad. He is credited with being the first person to plant this type of tobacco plant commercially in North America.

The export of this sweeter tobacco, beginning in 1612, helped turn the Virginia Colony into a profitable venture. Soon, Rolfe and others were exporting huge quantities of the new cash crop. New plantations began to spring up along the James River, where shippers could take advantage of the river's wharfs.

By 1621, however, the company was in deep trouble again. Unpaid dividends made future investors wary, and the company's debt had grown larger than ever. In March 1622, the company's and the colony's situation became even worse when the Powhatan Indians staged an uprising that wiped out one-fourth of the settlers. In 1624, the company lost its charter, and King James I made Virginia a royal colony, to be administered by a governor appointed by the king.

See also: Business Operations; England; Jamestown, Virginia; New England; Plymouth Company; Smith, John; Thirteen Colonies; Tobacco.

FURTHER READING

Grizzard, Frank, and D. Boyd Smith. *Jamestown Colony: A Political, Social, and Cultural History.* Santa Barbara, Cal.: ABC-CLIO, 2007.

Sakuri, Gail. *The Jamestown Colony.* New York: The Children's Press, 2007.

H–L

M

Magellan, Ferdinand (1480–1521)

Portuguese leader of a Spanish expedition to find a westward route to the Spice Islands—an island group also known as the Moluccas—in 1519. Pepper, cloves, ginger, cinnamon, and nutmeg brought high prices in European markets because these substances could be found only in India, Ceylon, and the Spice Islands, which were off the coast of Southeast Asia. Many explorers, including Magellan, set out to find sailing routes from Europe to the Indies that were shorter than the route around the southern tip of Africa.

Ferdinand Magellan was born in Sabrosa, Portugal, in 1480, to Pedro Ruy de Magalhães and Alda de Mezquita. He had one brother and two sisters. The family was a noble one; its origins were in the mountainous Traz-Os-Montes region of Portugal, a place described as having a "gloomy grandeur." Ferdinand Magellan likely spent his early youth in these mountains, developing a taste for exploration, a sound body, and an adventurous, determined spirit. At the age of 10, he was sent to Lisbon, where he became a page at the Portuguese royal court. His education was overseen by Queen Leonor (r. 1518–1521), who is also known as Eleanor of Habsburg.

ADVENTURE IN THE INDIES

In 1505, at the age of 25, Magellan joined Francisco d'Almeida's expedition to the Portuguese colony in India. Almeida's mission was to be **viceroy** of the colony and establish the rule of law. He set sail from Lisbon on March 25, 1505, with at least 20 ships and no fewer than 2,400 soldiers, sailors, and merchants.

Little is known of Magellan's participation in Almedia's colonization of the eastern African coast and India. In October 1505, the expedition took over the town of Kannur, on the western coast of India, and built a fortress called Fort Saint Angelo. The majority of Almeida's fleet then continued onward to the town of Kochi, leaving Almeida's son, Dom Lourenço, in charge at Kannur.

Lourenço was informed that the Indians were gathering a fleet in Calicut, a city further south. On March 16, 1506, a battle took place between 209 Indian ships and a fleet of 11 Portuguese vessels. Amazingly, the Portuguese won. They did this by successfully capturing the two largest ships in the Indian fleet. Magellan was injured during the battle; eventually, after he recovered, he was sent to Sofala, a town on the eastern coast of African in what is today Mozambique. In the three years that followed this victory, the Portuguese suffered many defeats. Dom Lourenço was killed, and

Almeida gathered a fleet to avenge the death of his son. Magellan joined in this attack and was wounded again.

In August 1509, Magellan joined an expedition of four ships that sailed from Kochi to Malacca, in Malaysia. Also onboard with Magellan was Francisco Serrão, who became one of Magellan's best friends. The expedition arrived at Malacca on September 11, 1509. The Portuguese were greeted kindly, but only because the king of Malacca needed time to plan his attack on the Portuguese ships.

The locals lured the majority of the Portuguese sailors to the shore. Luckily, however, the Europeans realized the danger they were in before the attack began. Magellan, who had gone ashore, went back to the fleet's flagship to warn its captain, Sequeira. Magellan arrived in time to tell Sequeira that he was about to be attacked. Magellan then returned to shore to help save the sailors who were under attack there, including his friend Serrão. The Portuguese failed to rescue a number of men who were taken captive, and Sequeira returned to India with only three of his original ships. Because of his bravery, Magellan was promoted to the rank of captain in 1510.

THE GREAT EXPEDITION

Magellan returned to Portugal in June 1512 and petitioned the king to send an expedition westward in search of a sea route to the Indies. Magellan's petition was rejected. In 1517, he took his proposal to the Spanish monarch, Charles V (r. 1516–1556). The Spanish king provided Magellan with 270 men and 5 ships—the *Trinidad*, the *San*

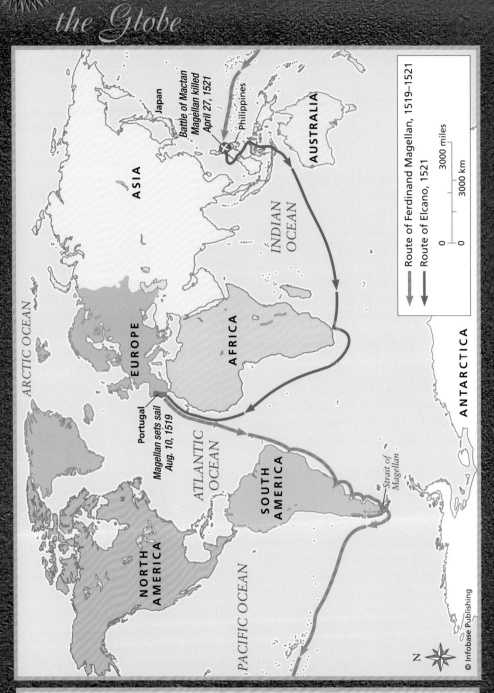

Magellan Circumnavigates the Globe

Route of Ferdinand Magellan, 1519–1521
Route of Elcano, 1521

0   3000 miles
0   3000 km

ARCTIC OCEAN

ASIA

Japan

Battle of Mactan
Magellan killed
April 27, 1521

Philippines

AUSTRALIA

INDIAN OCEAN

EUROPE

AFRICA

Portugal
Magellan sets sail
Aug. 10, 1519

ATLANTIC OCEAN

SOUTH AMERICA

Strait of Magellan

NORTH AMERICA

PACIFIC OCEAN

ANTARCTICA

N

© Infobase Publishing

Ferdinand Magellan's expedition was the first to sail around the globe, providing proof that the earth is round. Five ships set sail from Spain in 1519, but only one reached home. Magellan himself was killed in the Battle of Mactan in the Philippine Islands in April 1521.

Antonio, the *Concepción*, the *Victoria*, and the *Santiago*.

Magellan's fleet left from Spain on September 20, 1517. The ships were pursued by Portuguese ships that were under orders to stop Magellan from assisting Spain in finding its own route to the Spice Islands. Magellan and his men evaded the Portuguese ships and made their first stop in the Canary Islands. From there, they sailed on to Cape Verde, also off the west coast of Africa, and then westward toward Brazil, in the Americas.

Magellan's original Portuguese crew had been exchanged for a crew of Spaniards before his fleet was allowed to set sail. Many of his captains, however, were still Portuguese. Ironically, Magellan's own countrymen, the captains of the *San Antonio*, the *Concepción,* and the *Victoria*, were plotting a **mutiny.** The plotting of Juan de Cartagena, captain of the *San Antonio*, was discovered as the fleet sailed for Brazil. Magellan had his mutinous captain imprisoned on the *Victoria*.

On December 13, 1519, Magellan's fleet arrived off the coast of Rio de Janeiro, Brazil. The ships stocked up on food and water and set sail down the eastern South American coast in search of a route across the continent. In March 1520, they reached a harbor that they named Puerto San Julian, in the Patagonia region of present-day Argentina. While the fleet was at Puerto San Julian, Juan de Cartegena attempted a second mutiny. To regain control, Magellan marooned Cartegena of the coast of Patagonia in what is today Argentina. Magellan also had Gaspar de Quesada, a fellow mutineer

and captain of the *Concepción*, beheaded and **drawn and quartered** for his part in the revolt. The majority of the Spanish crew remained loyal to Magellan.

While most of the fleet stayed in port at San Julian, the *Santiago* was sent out to scout farther down the coast. In May, the *Santiago* was wrecked in bad weather, but the crew managed to trek back to Puerto San Julian. In August, Magellan took the remaining four ships south., He eventually sailed into the area now named the **Straits** of Magellan. From their ships, Magellan's men could see campfires along the coast. They named the area Tierra del Fuego, meaning "land of fire."

It took Magellan's fleet 38 days to navigate the straits. During that time, the captain of the *San Antonio* decided to return to Spain rather than continue into the unknown ocean that lay ahead, with no idea of how long the expedition's supplies would last. Because the captain of the *San Antonio* took most of the fleet's existing food and supplies with him, the remaining men were forced to hunt and fish to survive. On November 28, Magellan's fleet reached the ocean that he named Pacific for its calm waters.

On January 24, 1521, the fleet found a small, uninhabited island that they named Saint Paul. It offered little in the way of fresh food, however. On March 6, the three remaining ships, the *Trinidad*, the *Victoria*, and the *Concepción*, reached Guam and the Marianas, islands in the central Pacific. By the time they reached these islands, the men were starving. They had eaten the leather from the ship's rigging, rats, and sawdust. Because their diet lacked fresh fruits and vegetables, many of the men came down with scurvy, a disease caused by a lack of vitamin C. Among the symptoms of scurvy are bleeding and open sores.

From Guam, Magellan sailed west and slightly south. He landed in what is today the Philippines on March 28. Only 150 of his men were still alive. Here, Magellan became friends with Rajah Humabon, ruler of Cebu. Magellan converted the king to Christianity and was convinced to lead an attack against Humabon's enemy Lapu-Lapu, on the island of Mactan.

Magellan was killed in the Battle of Mactan, on April 27, 1521. One of his crew reported that he was first cut in the leg, which caused him to fall. The enemy forces then attacked with iron and bamboo spears "and ran him through—our mirror, our light, our comforter, our true guide—until they killed him."

THE RETURN TO SPAIN

The battle left the expedition with only about 100 men, enough to crew two ships. The *Concepción* was therefore burned at sea. The two remaining ships reached the Spice Islands in November. The ships departed laden with spices, and each took a different route to try to reach Spain. The *Trindad* headed east, back across the Pacific. It was captured by the Portuguese. The *Victoria* headed west, through the Indian Ocean, around the Cape of Good Hope, and up the west coast of Africa. Twenty of the 47 crew died of starvation, and another 13 were left behind in Cape Verde. On September 6, 1522, the *Victoria*

and its 18 remaining crewmen arrived in Seville, Spain. It was the first ship to **circumnavigate** the globe.

On hearing of Magellan's death, the king of Portugal ordered the Magellan family crest to be taken from his house in Sabrosa as punishment for his having aided the Spanish crown in its pursuit of riches in the Indies. Despite the fact that it was common for explorers to seek favor in foreign courts, Magellan was labeled a traitor by both his king and his fellow citizens. For many years, historians treated him as a villain. Having been stripped of any honors, Magellan's only living relative fled from Portugal. Magellan's family home eventually fell into ruin.

See also: Spain; Portugal.

FURTHER READING
Bergreen, Laurence. *Over the Edge of the World: Magellan's Terrifying Circumnavigation of the Globe.* New York: Harper Perennial, 2004.

M

Marquette, Jacques (1637–1675), and Louis Joliet (1645–1700)

First European explorers to map the northern portion of the Mississippi River. Marquette and Joliet lived in the **colony** of New France, around the Great Lakes region of present-day Michigan and southern Ontario. Like many explorers in America, they were searching for the **Northwest Passage,** a mythical water route to the Pacific Ocean.

A MISSIONARY IN NEW FRANCE

Jacques Marquette was born in Laon, France. As a boy, he attended a school run by Jesuit priests. At the age of 17, he joined their order. From 1654 to 1666, Marquette continued his studies and taught in the French city of Reims. In 1666, he was recruited as a missionary and sent to France's colony in America. When he arrived, he spent two years studying local Indian customs and languages. In 1668, he established a mission among the Ottawa people at Sault Sainte Marie in present-day Ontario. A year later, Marquette moved to the St. Esprit Mission on Lake Superior, where he worked among the Huron.

During this time, the Huron were attacked by the Lakota. The Huron escaped to the east and built a new settlement between Lake Michigan and Lake Huron. Marquette followed the Huron to continue his ministry and founded the St. Ignace mission in 1671. Because of the move, Marquette was introduced to a new group of Indians who spoke of a "big river," or *mississippi*, as it was called in their language. Marquette believed that this river might be the Northwest Passage, and he asked the governor general of New France for permission to search for it.

JOLIET

Louis Joliet was born in 1645 near Quebec City in the colony of New France. Like Marquette, he attended a school run by Jesuits and began studying to be a priest. In 1667, at age 22, he changed his mind and dropped out of the school.

Joliet loved to draw, and his abilities led him to drawing maps. This activity fueled his desire to explore. He soon joined his brothers as a fur trapper. In 1669, he was hired as a professional explorer by the French colonial government. In 1670, Joliet established a trading post in Sault Sainte Marie, in present-day Michigan. He traded weapons and other supplies for beaver furs, which were highly prized in France.

EXPLORING THE MISSISSIPPI

Governor General Comte de Frontenac granted Marquette permission to explore the "great river" and ordered Joliet to accompany him. On May 13, 1673, Marquette, Joliet, and five others left the mission of St. Ignace, at Michilimakinac on the northern tip of Lake Michigan. They paddled out in two birchbark canoes.

The explorers gathered as much information as they could from the surrounding Indians. The men traced out a rough map and marked where they believed different rivers and villages would be. Marquette saw the journey not only as a scientific exploration but also as an opportunity to spread Christianity to the Indians.

The first tribe Marquette and Joliet encountered was the Menominee. Marquette told the Menominee of his quest to travel down the Mississippi, and the men of the tribe tried to convince him to turn around. They said that the Frenchmen would meet dangerous people who would kill them without reason. They warned further of monsters that would swallow their boats whole. Marquette was grateful for the advice but said that saving the souls of the Indians he would meet was worth the risk. The expedition left the Menominee and headed toward the village of Maskoutens, where members of the Miami, Maskouten, and Kikabou tribes lived.

Marquette and Joliet arrived at Maskoutens on June 7, and the priest was pleased to see that a Christian cross stood in the center of the village. The Indians regularly received instruction from a Father Alloues, who had set up his mission in Maskoutens.

On June 10, after saying a prayer with the Indians, the expedition departed. Marquette and Joliet took two guides with them from the Miami tribe, men who could show them the way through the marshes to the Wisconsin River. From the Wisconsin River, they could reach the Mississippi.

The Mississippi at Last On June 17, 40 **leagues,** or 138 miles (222 kilometers), down the Wisconsin River, Marquette and Joliet came to the Mississippi. The river was 19 **fathoms,** or 114 feet (34.7 meters), deep and moved slowly because of its great depth. Marquette wrote in his journal that the land was full of deer and cattle. There were forests of oak and walnut, and vines grew in abundance.

As the explorers paddled down the Mississippi, the landscape changed. There were fewer forests and fewer animals. Their canoes were hit by large catfish, which the Frenchmen had never seen. Marquette also wrote of finding "wild cattle," or American bison.

An Encounter with the Illinois The party traveled 60 leagues, or 207 miles (333 kilometers), down the Mississippi before it found any evidence of other humans. The village the explorers discovered belonged to the Illinois people. The encounter was friendly, and Marquette was given a peace pipe, or *calumet*. The calumet is greatly honored among many Indiann tribes, and displaying it can allow one to walk safely among his enemies. The gift was meant as protection against the more dangerous tribes farther down the river.

Marquette and Joliet left the Illinois village near the end of June. The expedition next encountered the Missouri, a river with waters that were muddy and undrinkable. The party did not explore the Missouri beyond its mouth, despite the fact that Marquette believed that it would be a more likely route to the Pacific than the Mississippi. Instead, the expedition continued southward, eventually coming to the village of Akamsea, of the Quapaw tribe, near the Arkansas River. Here, they were told that the sea was only 10 days away. The Quapaw also said that Europeans lived in that direction. Marquette and Joliet assumed that these Europeans were the Spanish.

The Return Home Rather than risk capture and death at the hands of the Spanish, the Frenchmen decided to turn back. On July 17, they headed home. Thanks to the advice of local Indians, they paddled back on the Illinois River. The return trip was nearly a month shorter.

Jacques Marquette elected to stay at St. Francis Xavier, a mission in Green Bay, in what is now Wisconsin. Louis Joliet returned to Quebec to report on the expedition.

FOLLOWING THE EXPEDITION
In 1675, Marquette headed west to an area in present-day Illinois known as Starved Rock. There, he preached at the Grand Village of the Illinois and celebrated Mass. On his return

trip to his mission at St. Ignace, he died of illness near what is now Ludington, Michigan. In 1677, the Indians from St. Ignace returned to the site of his burial, dug up his body, and returned him to the mission with great ceremony.

In 1705, St. Ignace was set afire, and abandoned as it burned. The mission and Marquette's remains were lost until 1877, when the mission building's foundations were discovered during land excavation. A monument now stands on the site.

Louis Joliet's return to Quebec proved troublesome. His canoe overturned, and two of his comrades died. All of his notes from the expedition were lost, and he had to give his report from memory. After his return, he married Claire-Francoise Bissot. In 1697, he was granted land and a minor aristocratic title. Joliet died in 1700 while traveling to one of his properties.

See also: Native Americans; New France; Quebec; Spain.

FURTHER READING
Marquette, Jacques. *Marquette's First Voyage, 1673–1677: Travels and Explorations of the Jesuit Missionaries in New France.* Oaksdale, Wash.: Ye Galleon Press, 2001.

Maryland Act of Toleration

See Thirteen Colonies.

Mayflower, The

Ship that brought the Pilgrims, also known as English Separatists, to Plymouth, Massachusetts, where they started a **colony.** The *Mayflower* left Southampton, England on September 6, 1620, carrying 102 passengers and a crew of about 25 or 30.

The group originally planned to land in the area of what is present-day New York, where they had obtained permission to settle from the London Company, which was authorized to colonize that region. Fierce winter storms blew the ship off course and too far north, however. After an exhausting 66-day journey, the tiny ship reached what is today Provincetown, Massachusetts, on Cape Cod.

The exact dimensions of the *Mayflower* are unknown, but it was likely between 90 feet (27.4m) and 100 feet (30.4 m) long and 25 feet (7.6 m) wide. The ship's captain, Christopher Jones, owned the ship with some business partners. The ship was used most often for trading English goods with the French. The ship's historic 1620 voyage was its first and only one to the Americas.

REACHING AMERICA
When the Pilgrims reached the New England coast, which had been explored earlier by Captain John Smith, they realized that they did not have the right to settle in the area. Despite this knowledge, the *Mayflower* anchored in Provincetown Harbor on November 11, 1620. While still aboard the ship, to establish laws for their new colony, the colonists drafted a document known as the Mayflower Compact. All 41 of the adult men on board, Pilgrims as well as crew, signed the document.

Unsure of where to settle, the crew and the Pilgrims lived onboard the ship and sent out parties to explore the coast. Finally, in December 1620, John Bradford, the Pilgrims'

The Mayflower Compact

The Pilgrims and crew of the *Mayflower* set up a government based on a document that they wrote aboard the ship. It was the first document of its kind in what would become the United States. This agreement, known as the Mayflower Compact, set up a government that was to operate according to rules established by those who were to be governed. This document is, therefore, the first example of democracy in the Americas.

In the name of God, Amen. We, whose names are underwritten, the Loyal Subjects of our dread Sovereign Lord, King James, by the Grace of God, of England, France and Ireland, King, Defender of the Faith, e&. Having undertaken for the Glory of God, and Advancement of the Christian Faith, and the Honour of our King and Country, a voyage to plant the first colony in the northern parts of Virginia; do by these presents, solemnly and mutually in the Presence of God and one of another, covenant and combine ourselves together into a civil Body Politick, for our better Ordering and Preservation, and Furtherance of the Ends aforesaid; And by Virtue hereof to enact, constitute, and frame, such just and equal Laws, Ordinances, Acts, Constitutions and Offices, from time to time, as shall be thought most meet and convenient for the General good of the Colony; unto which we promise all due submission and obedience. In Witness whereof we have hereunto subscribed our names at Cape Cod the eleventh of November, in the Reign of our Sovereign Lord, King James of England, France and Ireland, the eighteenth, and of Scotland the fifty-fourth. Anno Domini, 1620.

M

leader, chose a place on the coast for the settlement. According to tradition, Bradford set foot on Plymouth Rock, in what is today the town of Plymouth, Massachusetts.

The winter of 1620–1621 was harsh, and supplies were low. Despite having chosen a location for the col-ony, the Pilgrims and the crew stayed aboard the *Mayflower* until spring. As the weather warmed, the colonists began to build huts on shore, and on March 21, 1621, the Pilgrims left the *Mayflower*. The ship departed for home on April 5, 1621, and reached England on May 6. Christopher Jones,

Used most often as a cargo ship, the *Mayflower* provided uncomfortable accommodations for the Pilgrims. After a 66-day voyage across the Atlantic Ocean to reach Plymouth colony, the ship finally stopped at the tip of Cape Cod, in what is today Massachusetts.

the *Mayflower*'s captain, died in March 1622.

See also: England; New England; Plymouth Company; Smith, John; Thirteen Colonies.

Further Reading

Johnson, Caleb. *The Mayflower and Her Passengers*. Philadelphia, Pa.: Xlibris. 2006.

Philbrick, Nathaniel. *Mayflower: A Story of Courage, Community, and War*. New York: Penguin, 2007.

Mayflower Compact, The

See *Mayflower*, The.

Mercantilism

An economic theory popular among the European powers in the **colonial era**–the sixteenth through the eighteenth centuries. According to the theory of mercantilism, the prosperity of a nation depended on the amount of capital, or money, that it held in its treasury. Believers in mercantilism also claimed that the amount of world trade was unchangeable. Thus, according to mercantilist thought, for one nation to grow richer, other nations had to grow poorer.

Belief in the theory of mercantilism was a major reason why the European nations of Spain, England, France, and the Netherlands sent explorers to the Americas and to Asia in search of gold and other riches. By adding gold, silver, and other assets to the national treasury, each nation believed that it was increasing its own wealth and power. Each nation worked to maintain a positive **balance of trade**—that is, to **export** more than it **imported.** Each nation also strove to achieve economic self-sufficiency by decreasing its dependence on trade with other nations.

Another key characteristic of mercantilism was the establishment of overseas colonies. These colonies were to provide raw materials to the parent country, which would use the materials to produce manufactured goods. In turn, the manufactured goods would be sold to the colonies—a captive market for the parent county. Sea power was essential to a mercantilist economic policy. If a nation had its own powerful merchant fleet, it would not need to use ships of other nations to conduct its trade. This would help the parent nation become even more self-sufficient. In addition, an impressive fleet added to a nation's prestige and military power.

Mercantilism involved a great deal of government control of the nation's economy. In general, governments imposed high **tariffs,** or taxes, on imported goods to make them more expensive. At the same time, however, taxes on raw materials imported from the nation's own colonies were kept low.

The primary mercantilist nations were Spain, France, and England. Spain exercised strict control over its colonies and merchants. In France, Jean-Baptiste Colbert, the chief financial minister of King Louis XIV (r. 1643–1715), prohibited the export of cash and imposed high tariffs on all foreign-made goods. The English Parliament passed laws that allowed the government to regulate business hours, award business monopolies, and fix prices.

Mercantilist polices came to an end in the late 1700s. In 1776, the economist Adam Smith published a book called *The Wealth of Nations*, in which he described how a **laissez-faire,** or free enterprise, economic system works. In brief, Smith showed that trade benefits both parties. He also pointed out that **specialization in production** allows for **economies of scale.** This improves efficiency and growth, thereby creating more wealth.

See also: England; France; London Company; Spain.

FURTHER READING
Ekelund, Robert B., and Robert D. Tollison. *Politicized Economies: Monarchy, Monopoly, and Mercantilism.* College Station: Texas A&M University Press, 1997.

Missionaries

See Ferdinand and Isabella; France; Marquette, Jacques, and Louis Joliet; Quebec.

N

Native Americans

The original inhabitants of the Americas. Many scholars believe that the Americas remained uninhabited by humans until between 25,000 and 40,000 years ago. According to most scholars, at that time, nomadic peoples from Asia crossed into North America by means of a land bridge that once connected the two continents.

In the centuries that followed, the earliest Americans adapted to many new environments and established varied and thriving cultures throughout North and South America. By the 1500s, **native peoples** lived in every environment in the Americas. Estimates of the number of Native Americans populating the two continents at this time vary widely—from about 1 million to more than 10 million.

More than 600 languages had developed among the native peoples.

CULTURE

In general, although several different cultures emerged, many similarities existed among the various Native American groups. The organization of many Native American societies was based on the tribe. Tribal members spoke the same language and shared customs and beliefs. Tribes were made up of several bands; each band consisted of several families who occupied a particular area.

The clan was also a familiar feature of many Native American tribes. A clan was similar to an extended family—a household that may include parents, children, grandparents, aunts, uncles, and cousins—who claimed descent from a common ancestor. Clans sometimes included adopted members as well. The clan was an important element in tribal society because outside of the immediate family, the clan was the basic unit of native life.

The leaders of many tribes were sachems, or chiefs. These chiefs gained their positions as political or ceremonial leaders either by election or by inheritance, depending on the traditions of the tribe. Many tribes, however, often shared decision-making.

Religious Beliefs A number of Native American cultures developed complex religious beliefs. Most Native Americans believed in the power of supernatural beings—spirits—that resided in all things. The Native Americans often tried to understand and use this power through visions or dreams, which were thought to be sacred. Shamans, or religious leaders, were believed to have close contact with the spirit world and could do such things as cure sickness. The importance of shamans as ceremonial and religious leaders often gave them political influence, as well.

ECONOMIES

The economies of the earliest Native American societies were based largely on hunting, fishing, and the gathering of plants for food. As later cultures evolved, the earlier ways were adapted to meet new or changing environments. Food, clothing, and shelter remained the major concern of all groups. An important change took place in some areas as **agriculture,** or farming, developed.

By about 1500, farming existed in many areas throughout the Americas. It varied from small-scale, subsistence farming—the minimum needed to support one family—to large-scale agriculture that was dependent on **irrigation.** In North America alone, native farmers grew more than 100 plants, including modern staple crops such as corn and potatoes.

EASTERN WOODLANDS CULTURE

The Europeans who explored the coasts and waterways of North America and later colonized the area encountered native peoples from the Eastern Woodlands culture. The peoples who lived in this vast area, which extended from the Atlantic Coast west to the Mississippi River Valley and from the Gulf of Mexico north to Canada, shared many cultural characteristics.

The region contained dense forests, scattered grasslands, fertile river valleys, and rushing streams. This favorable environment yielded abundant sources of food. The native peoples of this region had a wide knowledge of the lands on which they lived. By moving from place to place during the different seasons of the year to find food, the Eastern Woodlands peoples enjoyed a diverse diet. To meet their food needs, they hunted deer and small game; fished; gathered shellfish; and collected nuts, wild seeds, berries, and plants. They also engaged in such practices as tapping maple trees for sugar.

Farming Agriculture also added to the food stores of the Eastern Woodlands people. Maize, or corn, which had originated in what is today Mexico, became the major crop. Beans and squash also were key crops. Slash-and-burn agriculture was used. In this method, trees and brush were cut down and burned, and the ash that remained enriched the soil. This fertilization method lasted only a short time, however, and as old fields began to yield less, new fields had to be cleared. As a result, slash-and-burn farmers moved continually.

Early Cultures The development and spread of agriculture resulted in two complex cultures in the Eastern Woodlands before 1400. These were the Hopewell culture, which flourished from about 200 B.C.E. to C.E. 200, and the Mississippian culture, which reached its peak around C.E. 1200. Large, well-organized villages characterized both of these societies. These cultures are sometimes called Mound Builders because they built large, earthen mounds that served many purposes.

The Mississippians were the last group of Mound Builders. They lived along the Mississippi and Ohio rivers. Some of their towns were small, but others housed as many as 20,000 people.

One of the largest Mississippian settlements was the city of Cahokia, in what is today southern Illinois. Around the center of the city, which covered about six square miles (15.5 square kilometers), was a wall of logs standing on end and coated with clay. This stockade enclosed about 300 acres (121 hectares). Within the wall were houses, a marketplace, and many mounds.

The marketplace was one of the most important places in the city. There, people traded salt, furs, lumps of copper, and sharp-edged stones used for hoes. Artists traded their pottery and carved shells.

The many mounds of Cahokia were used in different ways. Corn and other crops that were grown along a nearby river were stored in some small mounds. Other mounds were platforms for the houses of important people. The largest mound, which stands 100 feet (30 meters) high and covers 15 acres (6 hectares), was probably used for religious ceremonies.

In about C.E. 1600, the inhabitants deserted the city of Cahokia. Most likely, the people left because the fields along the rivers could no longer provide enough food.

Near what is today Natchez, Mississippi, French fur traders found a large Mississippian settlement in 1704. According to the French, the Natchez group was divided into several classes. Heading the group was a ruler known as the Great Sun. He held the power of life and death over his people and was their chief priest. Below him were the nobles and a class called the "honored people." Members of the lower class—farmers, soldiers, and slaves—could become members of the honored people by doing some daring deed or fighting bravely in war.

THE IROQUOIS

Most of the Native American groups that lived in the Eastern Woodlands were descendents of the Mound Builders. Among the most famous and powerful were the Iroquois, who lived in parts of the present-day states of New York and Pennsylvania, as well as in Canada. The Iroquois lived in dwellings called **longhouses** that were grouped together in towns. Around the towns were stockade fences, and beyond the fences were fields of corn, beans, squash, and other vegetables.

A longhouse had no windows or chimneys, but it had a doorway at each end. A single longhouse housed as many as 12 families. Each family lived in part of the house, on one side of a central hall. A family cooked in the central hall on an open fire that was shared with the family that lived directly across the hall.

Women in Iroquois Society
In Iroquois society, the women of the family owned everything, including the longhouses and the fields. Iroquois children took their mothers' names, not their fathers'. In addition, families traced their history through mothers. When two people married, the husband went to live in his wife's longhouse. Iroquois women held much governing power and chose all the

delegates to the tribal council, who were men, including the tribe's chief.

The Iroquois League
In the 1500s, several Iroquois groups, or nations, were at war with one another. To put an end to this fighting among themselves, in 1570, five nations banded together to form the Iroquois League. These nations were the Mohawk, Oneida, Onondaga, Cayuga, and Seneca. A sixth Iroquois nation, the Tuscarora, joined the league in 1722. The league worked to find peaceful ways to settle disagreements among the Iroquois peoples and to form a stronger defense against their enemies.

A council of 50 men called peace chiefs governed the league. They were chosen as delegates for life by the women of the member nations and met each summer to discuss disputes among members. They also sometimes planned warfare against other groups. The Iroquois League lasted until 1784.

OTHER NATIVE AMERICAN CULTURES

Farther south, in what is today central Mexico, Spanish explorers encountered the vast Aztec empire. When the Spanish reached Tenochtitlán, the Aztec capital, in 1519, it was larger than any city in Europe at the time. Despite its size, power, and great wealth, the Aztec empire fell to Spanish **conquistadors** in 1521.

In South America, the mighty Inca empire also fell to Spanish conquistadors. Stretching along the Pacific coast of the continent, the Inca empire's government was highly organized, and the empire's ruler—called the Inca—held complete power over his subjects. The Spanish arrived in Inca lands in 1532, and the empire fell the following year.

See also: Aztec empire; *The Diversity of Native America* in the "Viewpoints" section; French and Indian War; Inca Empire; New France; Thirteen Colonies.

FURTHER READING

Milner, George R. *The Moundbuilders: Ancient Peoples of Eastern North America.* New York: Thames & Hudson, 2005.

Waldman, Carl. *Atlas of the North American Indian.* New York: Facts On File, 2008.

Wilcox, Charlotte. *The Iroquois.* Minneapolis, Minn.: Learner, 2006.

Netherlands

Small, seafaring nation located in northwestern Europe; an important colonial trading power. In the 1500s, Spain controlled the area that is today the Netherlands. In 1568, when King Philip II (r. 1556–1598) tried to suppress political and religious freedom in the region, a revolt broke out. It was led by the Dutch nobleman William I, Prince of Orange.

Under the Union of Utrecht (1579), the region's seven northern provinces became the United Provinces of the Netherlands. War between the United Provinces and Spain continued well into the seventeenth century, but in 1648, Spain finally recognized Dutch independence.

In 1602, the government of the Netherlands chartered the Dutch East India Company. The charter granted the company the sole rights, for a period of 21 years, to Dutch trade and navigation east of the Cape of Good Hope (at the southern tip of Africa)

and west of the Straits of Magellan (at the southern tip of South America). The directors of the company were given authority to establish forts, sign treaties, set up an army and navy, and wage defensive war. The company was founded as a **joint-stock company.**

In 1621, the Dutch West India Company was set up. This company was given a 25-year **monopoly** in those parts of the world that were not controlled by the East India Company: the Atlantic, the Americas, and the west coast of Africa. Soon, Dutch colonies and trading posts were established all over the globe, and by the end of the 1600s, the Netherlands was one of the great sea and colonial powers of Europe.

In 1603 and again in 1610, the Dutch unsuccessfully attacked Goa, on the west coast of India, the center of the Portuguese empire in Asia. The Dutch also tried but were also unable to capture the Portuguese colony of Macau, on the coast of China, the point from which Portugal monopolized the profitable China-Japan trade. In 1619, the Dutch captured Jakarta, in what is today Indonesia.

In 1639, the Japanese government's increasing suspicion of the Catholic Portuguese led to the Portuguese being thrown out of Japan. Under a new Japanese policy, the Dutch became the only European power authorized to trade in Japan. At first, the Dutch were confined to the port at Hirado. Then, from 1641, the Dutch were confined to the port at Deshima. Meanwhile, the Dutch fought to drive out the Portuguese from their trading posts in Asia. Malacca surrendered in 1641, Colombo

N

fell in 1656, and Ceylon succumbed in 1658.

By the middle of the seventeenth century, the Dutch had surpassed Portugal as the major power in the spice and silk trade with Asia. In 1652, the Dutch founded a colony at Cape Town, on the coast of South Africa. This colony served as a way station for Dutch ships on the route between Europe and Asia.

In the Atlantic region, the Dutch West India Company worked to take over Portugal's control of the sugar and slave trade. The ships of the company also attacked Spanish treasure fleets on their voyages home from Spain's American colonies.

The Dutch captured Bahia, on the northeastern coast of Brazil, in 1624 but held it for only a year before a joint Spanish-Portuguese expedition retook it. In 1630, the Dutch occupied the Portuguese settlement of Pernambuco in Brazil and during the next few years pushed inland. The Dutch then **annexed** the sugar plantations that surrounded Pernambuco. To supply the plantations with workers, in 1637, the Dutch launched an expedition from Brazil to capture the Portuguese slaving post of Elmina in Africa. In 1641, the Dutch successfully captured Portuguese settlements in Angola, on the west coast of Africa. By 1650, the Dutch West India Company was firmly in control of both the sugar and slave trades. The Dutch also occupied the Caribbean islands of Saint Maarten, Curaçao, and Aruba.

Dutch successes against the Portuguese in Brazil and Africa did not last for long, however. In 1645, the Portuguese settlers at Pernambuco in Brazil rebelled against their Dutch masters, and by 1654, the Dutch had been driven out. A Portuguese expedition was sent from Brazil to recapture the city of Luanda in Angola, and by 1648, the Dutch also were expelled from that region.

On the northeastern coast of North America, the Dutch West India Company took over Fort Orange, at Albany, on the Hudson River. In 1625, to protect its upriver position at Albany from the nearby English and French, the company founded the town of New Amsterdam at the mouth of the Hudson. The company also encouraged Dutch colonists to settle in the surrounding areas of Long Island and what is today New Jersey. In 1655, the nearby colony of New Sweden was taken over by the Dutch colony of New Netherland after the Dutch governor, Peter Stuyvesant, sent ships and soldiers to capture the Swedish outpost.

In 1664, the English took over the Dutch colony of New Netherland and renamed it New York. Over time, Dutch colonial power began to fade, although the Netherlands retained control of many of its Asian colonies until after World War II (1939–1945). The Netherlands still governs several islands in the Caribbean region.

See also: New Netherland; Portugal; Spain; Thirteen Colonies.

FURTHER READING
Rietburgen, Piet. *A Short History of the Netherlands.* Langley, B.C.: Vanderheide Publishing, 2004.

New England

Name given to the northernmost of England's thirteen **colonies** in North America. The colonies of Plymouth, Massachusetts, Rhode Island, Connecticut, and New Hampshire made up the area called New England. In 1691, Plymouth Colony was made a part of Massachusetts.

Explorers from several colonial powers, including France and the Netherlands, sailed the coastal area of the region. The English seafarer John Smith explored the shores of the region in 1614 and named the area New England. Smith praised the land and its rich forests in his account of his voyages, which he published in 1616 as *A Description of New England*.

NEW ENGLAND CONFEDERATION

In the early colonial years, the relationship between English settlers and the local Indian peoples alternated between peace and armed warfare. In 1643, six years after a bloody confrontation known as the Pequot War, the colonies of Massachusetts Bay, Plymouth, and Connecticut joined together in a loose compact called the New England Confederation.

The goal of this weak **confederation** was to coordinate mutual defense against possible attacks from the Indians. The confederation also sought to protect the English colonies from the Dutch in New Netherland to the west, the Spanish to the south, and the French to the north. In 1654, after Massachusetts refused to join the fight against New Netherland, the confederation grew weaker. It regained importance in 1676, however, during the conflict with the Indians known as King Philip's War. In 1684, the confederation disbanded.

DOMINION OF NEW ENGLAND

England's King James II (r. 1685–1688) attempted to exert royal control over the New England colonies. He especially wanted to enforce the 1651 Navigation Acts. These laws, passed by the British Parliament, required that all English trade be carried out on English ships. In 1686, the king established the Dominion of New England, an administrative union made up of all the New England colonies. In 1688, the colonies of New York and New Jersey, which had been seized from the Dutch in 1664, were added to the dominion.

Because the Dominion of New England was imposed by the king, it was highly unpopular among the colonists. The colonists believed that the establishment of the dominion went against the democratic tradition of the region. In 1689, after England's **Glorious Revolution** peacefully removed King James II from the throne, the colonists in Boston imprisoned the dominion's royal governor and other favorites of the king. The Dominion of New England came to an end.

FARMING AND INDUSTRY

New England's soil is thin and rocky. Because such soil needed constant attention, colonial farmers kept their plots small enough to be worked by a single family. Families usually produced enough grain and vegetables to feed themselves and their farm

A Description of New England

Captain John Smith sailed along the coast of what today is New England in 1614 and in 1616 published a book, *A Description of New England.* In this excerpt, he tells of his landing off the coast of New England and describes the crew's attempts to catch a whale.

In the moneth of Aprill, 1614. with two Ships from *London,* of a few Marchants, I chanced to arriue in *New-England,* a parte of *Ameryca,* at the Ile of *Monahiggan,* . . . our plot was there to take Whales and make tryalls of a Myne of Gold and Copper. If those failed, Fish and Furres was then our refuge, to make our selues [selfs] sauers [safer] howsoeuer: we found this Whale-fishing a costly conclusion: we saw many, and spent much time in chasing them; but could not Kill any: They beeing a kinde of Iubartes, and not the Whale that yeeldes Finnes and Oyle as wee expected. For our Golde, it was rather the Masters deuice to get a voyage that proiected it, then any knowledge hee had at all of any such matter. Fish & Furres was now our guard: & by our late arriual, and long lingring about the Whale, the prime of both those seasons were past ere wee perceiued it; we thinking that their seasons serued at all times: but wee found it otherwise; for, by the midst of Iune [June], the fishing failed. Yet in Iuly [July] and August some was taken, but not sufficient to defray so great a charge as our stay required. Of dry fish we made about 40000. . . .Whilest the sailers fished, my selfe with eight or nine others of them might best bee spared; Ranging the coast in a small boat, wee got for trifles neer 1100 Beuer [beaver] skinnes, 100 Martins, and neer as many Otters; and the most of them within the distance of twenty leagues.

animals. Sometimes, they had a small **surplus** that they could offer for sale.

Most New England farmers lived near a village or town. Indeed, life in New England centered around the area's towns. Farmers took advantage of common pastures to graze their cattle, and colonists lived near their churches and schools.

Lumbering and Shipbuilding Originally, thick forests covered much of New England. As the settlers cut down the forests to make way for farmland, mill owners built sawmills and sold the lumber, much of which was used to build and repair wooden ships. The growing New England fishing industry increased the demand for ships. Shipyards sprang up along the New England coast, from what is now Maine to Massachusetts. During the 1600s, the cities of Boston and Salem in Massachusetts became important shipbuilding centers.

Fishing and Whaling Fishing and whaling became important industries in New England. The coastal waters around New England and the Canadian island of Newfoundland teemed with cod and mackerel. After the fish were dried and packed, New Englanders shipped them to other mainland colonies, to the West Indies, and to Europe. Around 1715, whaling reached a new level. In that year, a fishing vessel was outfitted to pursue whales and tow them to shore. Sixty years later, more than 350 ships were in the whaling industry.

See also: England; Plymouth Company; Smith, John; Thirteen Colonies.

FURTHER READING
Lepore, Jill. *Encounters in the New World: A History in Documents.* New York. Oxford University Press, 2003.
Schultz, Eric B., and Michael J. Tougias. *King Philip's War: The History and Legacy of America's Forgotten War.* Woodstock, Vt.: Countryman Press, 2000.

New France

Name given to all colonial French land holdings in the Americas. After Spain's early successes in the Americas, other European nations grew more interested in exploration of the new lands. As early as 1504, French fishers were making regular trips to the abundant waters of the Grand Banks, off the coast of Newfoundland. At this time, rumors of a northern water route to Asia—the **Northwest Passage**—spread throughout France.

FIRST EXPLORATIONS

In 1524, Giovanni da Verrazano, an Italian navigator sailing for France, explored the eastern coast of North America from Newfoundland south to what is today North Carolina. Verrazano sailed across the mouth of the Hudson River, into Narragansett Bay in what is today Rhode Island, and along Cape Cod. He failed, however, to find the fabled Northwest Passage.

Jacques Cartier made voyages to North America in 1534 and 1535 with the hope of finding the mysterious Northwest Passage. He discovered the Gulf of St. Lawrence and the St. Lawrence River and sailed as far as the site of present-day Montreal. There, he came across impassible rapids, or rushing water, which he named the Lachine [China] Rapids.

In 1535, Cartier and his crew spent a bitter winter near the site of present-day Quebec. Six years later, Cartier returned with a larger expedition, including Jesuit priests, to Canada—the name the native people had given to the region of the St. Lawrence Valley. He still searched for the Northwest Passage and hoped to establish an outpost in the region, but he failed.

For the next 60 years, France was involved in a series of religious wars in Europe. As a result, the French showed little interest in further exploration or colonization in North America.

During the early 1600s, however, French explorations in North America were renewed. Over a period of 30 years, Samuel de Champlain made several voyages to the St. Lawrence Valley. Champlain did more than anyone else to firmly establish French influence in the area, which soon became known as New France.

In 1608, Champlain founded Quebec as a fur-trading post. He later established a profitable network with other fur-trading posts at Port Royal, Montreal, and Trois-Riviers. Champlain also developed friendly relations with many of the local Indians, including the Huron. Champlain made bitter enemies of the powerful Iroquois, however. The Iroquois later became **allies** of the English.

FURTHER EXPLORATION

Even as the fur trade boomed, the French continued to look for a way westward to Asia. In 1634, Jean Nicolet reached Green Bay, an arm of Lake Michigan, and traveled up the Fox River in what is today the state of Wisconsin. He reportedly carried a Chinese robe with him, expecting to reach Asia. Nicolet, however, found only more Indians, most likely the Winnebago.

Although Nicolet reported his finding of a portage—a path between rivers over which travelers could carry their boats—to a great river even farther west, the French did not immediately send other explorers to the area. About 40 years later, European fur traders, known as *coureurs de bois,* or "runners of the woods," traveled past Lake Huron.

GOVERNING NEW FRANCE

By 1660, the French—led by King Louis XIV (r. 1643–1715) and his powerful finance minister, Jean-Baptiste Colbert—took a greater interest in New France. In 1663, the region was named a royal province, and control of its affairs passed from private businesses to the French government. A powerful new political official, called the *intendant,* was appointed to head the government. In addition, a governing council was chosen to advise the new leader. For the first time, an efficient central government existed in New France. Around this same time, the French began to realize the importance of further settlement and exploration in North America if they were to secure their claims on the continent.

LATER EXPLORATIONS

In 1673, Louis Joliet, a fur trader, and Jacques Marquette, a Jesuit priest who spoke several native languages, explored the Fox, Wisconsin, and Mississippi rivers. The explorers traveled as far south as the Arkansas River, where they became convinced that the Mississippi continued to flow south into Spanish-held lands and emptied into the Gulf of Mexico.

During the next 10 years, more explorations were made in the Great Lakes region and in the lands to the south. A successful fur trader, René-Robert Cavelier, Sieur de La Salle, reached the mouth of the Mississippi River and claimed all the lands drained by the river for France. He called the land Louisiana, in honor of the French king, Louis XIV.

CHALLENGES TO NEW FRANCE

By 1700, the English, who also claimed parts of Canada, including the Hudson Bay region, were challenging French control of Canada. There, the English had established a profitable fur trade. During the next 60 years, disputes in Europe and in America led to several clashes between France and Great Britain.

See also: France; French and Indian War; Marquette, Jacques, and Louis Joliet; *The Opening of the Fur Trade* in the "Viewpoints" section; Quebec.

FURTHER READING

Chartrand, Rene. *The Forts of New France in Northeast America, 1600–1763.* Oxford, England: Osprey, 2008.

Worth, Richard. *Voices from Colonial America: New France 1534–1763.* Washington, D.C.: National Geographic Children's Books, 2007.

New Netherland

Located in the region of present-day New York, lands claimed and settled by the seafaring nation of the Netherlands. In the early 1600s, the Netherlands had begun to make plans to extend its trading network in Asia. In 1609, Dutch merchants hired the English navigator Henry Hudson to search for a **Northwest Passage** to Asia.

Hudson reached the coast of North America near what is today Maine. He then proceeded south as far as present-day Chesapeake Bay in Maryland. Determining that this waterway was not the Northwest Passage, Hudson turned around and sailed north. In the area of present-day New York City, he reached the mouth of the Hudson River, which later was named in his honor. Hudson claimed the land for the Netherlands and then sailed up the river to where the city of Albany now stands.

ESTABLISHING A COLONY

Dutch merchants soon took advantage of Hudson's explorations and established a profitable fur trade in the Hudson River Valley. In time, this area became known as New Netherland. In 1624, the Dutch built a trading post—Fort Orange—on the site of what today is Albany. The next year, the Dutch West India Company—a corporation that had been formed to oversee trade in New Netherland—founded the colonial settlement of New Amsterdam on the southern tip of Manhattan Island, at the mouth of the Hudson River. By the late 1620s, other discoveries enabled the Dutch to claim the entire stretch of Atlantic coast from the Connecticut River in the north to the Delaware Bay in the south.

The settlement of New Netherland was a slow process, however. The Dutch West India Company had hoped to populate the colony by granting large estates to wealthy individuals. In turn, these people would guarantee—at their own expense—to settle 50 families from the Netherlands in the estate areas within a few years. This was called the **patroon system.**

Dutch colonists established a number of other communities and trading posts throughout New Netherland. In 1655, Governor Peter Stuyvesant **annexed** a small Swedish colony located on nearby Delaware Bay. By

HISTORY MAKERS
Peter Stuyvesant (1592?–1672)

Peter Stuyvesant was the last Dutch governor of the colony of New Netherland. The exact year of Stuyvesant's birth is uncertain. Some sources say 1592; others place the date as late as 1612. Stuyvesant joined the military at an early age. He served in the West Indies and served as governor of the Dutch colony of Curaçao. During an unsuccessful attack on the Portuguese island of St. Martin, he was wounded and returned to Holland. There, the injury grew more serious, and his right leg was amputated. In 1646, he was appointed governor of New Netherland. He reached New Amsterdam, the colony's capital, on May 11, 1647.

Stuyvesant worked hard to improve conditions in the colony. Among his first proclamations were orders to enforce the rigid religious observance of Sunday and to prohibit the sale of liquor and firearms to the Indians. He also tried to protect the colony's **revenue** and increase its treasury by placing heavier taxes on imports. He called on builders to construct better houses and taverns, and he established a market and an annual cattle fair. A firm believer in education, Stuyvesant worked to found public schools. By 1661, New Amsterdam had one grammar school and two free elementary schools, as well as 28 licensed teachers.

Despite his efforts to improve the colony, Stuyvesant was not popular. He ruled the colony strictly and allowed no one to disagree with him. In addition, he was not tolerant of other religions, especially the Religious Society of Friends, known popularly as the Quakers.

After surrendering the colony to the English in 1664, Stuyvesant returned to the Netherlands to report on the situation. He then came back to New Amsterdam and settled on his large farm. He died in 1672 and is buried in a chapel in St. Mark's Church in-the-Bowery in New York City.

1660, however, only the settlement of New Amsterdam, which had a population of more than 1,000 at the time, flourished as a commerce center in the colony. Soon, New Netherland was challenged by England, a fast-growing colonial power in North America.

THE END OF NEW NETHERLAND

As England's North American colonies grew, the English began to look upon New Netherland as a threat. A chief concern was that the Dutch colony separated England's northern and southern colonies and blocked English colonial growth. The English feared possible Dutch moves northward and southward from New Netherland. Furthermore, Dutch control of the fur trade with the Indians along the Hudson River annoyed the English.

England's King Charles II (r. 1660–1685) decided to end Dutch rule in North America. In 1664, the king granted the land between the Connecticut and Delaware rivers to his brother, the Duke of York. Charles then sent an English fleet to the Hudson River. The fleet anchored near New Amsterdam, and the English demanded that the Dutch surrender the colony. Peter Stuyvesant, the governor, tried to rouse his people to fight the English but failed. Stuyvesant reluctantly surrendered without firing a shot. Both the colony and the city were renamed New York in honor of the Duke of York.

See also: Henry Hudson; Netherlands; New Sweden.

FURTHER READING
Gibson, Karen Bush. *New Netherland: The Dutch Settle the Hudson Valley.* Hockessin, Del.: Mitchell Lane Publishers, 2006.

New Spain

During the **colonial era,** Spanish **colonies** and possessions in the Americas. By 1541, Spain claimed vast parts of both North and South America.

Spain controlled nearly all of South America except Brazil, which Portugal had claimed first. The Spanish also held all of Mexico and Central America. Included in New Spain were the islands of the West Indies and the lands from Florida westward to California across the southern part of what is today the United States.

SPANISH COLONIAL POLICY

The new lands in the Western Hemisphere posed many problems for the **monarchs** of Spain. Originally, King Ferdinand and Queen Isabella had supported the voyages of Columbus to establish trading outposts to Asia. With the unexpected discovery of two vast continents, however, Spain

was unprepared to rule a huge empire. Plans had to be made to govern the new lands and peoples conquered by Spain. In addition, policies had to be established for the trade that had sprung up across the Atlantic.

In 1503—barely more than a decade after Columbus's first voyage to the Americas—the Spanish crown established two key policies that greatly influenced the new Spanish colonies. First, the crown set up a board to regulate and monopolize trade with Spanish America. The monopoly assured that every ounce of gold and silver mined in the Americas would be sent to Spain. Under this economic policy of mercantilism, Spain became the richest nation in Europe. Furthermore, Spanish colonists could only buy goods brought to the Americas by Spanish merchants in Spanish ships.

In addition to the trading monopoly, a system of *encomiendas* was set up in Spanish America. An encomienda was a piece of land that was "entrusted," along with the native peoples living on it, to a **conquistador** or other Spanish colonist. The land and the native peoples on it were not owned by the Spaniards to whom the land was entrusted; instead, the lands were held in trust for the colonists by the king.

The *encomenderos,* as the new Spanish lords were called, were required to protect the Indians in their trust and to teach them the Roman Catholic faith. In return, each encomendero could demand tribute or labor from the native peoples on his land. Using this system, a critical labor shortage in the fields and in the mines could be eased.

The encomienda system led to the enslavement of the Indians in many Spanish lands. The Catholic Church became the most vocal opponent of these abuses. As early as 1512, laws were passed in Spain to protect the native peoples of the Americas.

One of the most outspoken churchmen to condemn the treatment of the native peoples was Bartolomé de Las Casas. In the 1540s, he managed to gain royal support for reforms that eased the plight of some enslaved Indians. Too often, however, the laws were ignored by the wealthy and powerful. The encomienda system was not outlawed until the 1700s.

SPANISH COLONIES AND SLAVERY

Blacks first came to the Caribbean in 1502, but these men were likely freeborn Christian Spaniards. Around 1510, however, trade in African slaves flourished as colonists demanded more laborers. By the mid-1500s, at least 10,000 slaves were being imported to New Spain each year.

LATER CHANGES

In 1535, a new political structure was set up in Spain's colonial empire to replace the rule and influence of the conquistadors. **Vice-royalties** were established in what is today Mexico—then called New Spain—as well as in Peru in South America. **Viceroys** were appointed to rule as representatives of the king. Courts, called *audiencias*, were also set up.

In what is today the United States, Spanish settlement took a different pattern than it did in Mexico or Peru. The Roman Catholic Church pioneered in many areas. During the 1600s and 1700s, Spanish priests established missions along the Gulf of Mexico and along the coast of California. These missions not only taught the native peoples the Catholic faith but also showed them new methods of farming and new crafts. *Presidios*, or forts, also were built near many of the missions in North America to protect the missions.

DECLINE OF SPANISH POWER

Gold and silver continued to pour into Spain throughout the 1500s and early 1600s. By 1650, however, the rich mines of the Spanish colonies were nearly empty. The decline in shipments of precious metals was combined with a decrease in Spain's political and military power. Several other factors also led to Spain's decline at this time.

Economic Issues First, Spain failed to build up a strong system of trade. In theory, the gold and silver that were shipped to Spain from the colonies would be used to purchase goods made in Spain that would be sent back to the Americas. In practice, however, the system operated differently and caused economic problems for Spain. Most of the newfound wealth became concentrated in the hands of a few people—the Spanish monarch and the upper classes. These individuals were unwilling or unlikely to start new businesses. In addition, the flood of gold and silver caused high **inflation** in Spain. In Madrid, the capital, the price of grain rose more than twice as fast as the wages of workers in the city.

New Spanish industries failed to develop because it was easier to buy goods from other countries—primarily from countries in northern Europe and from England. By the early 1600s, more than 90 percent of the goods shipped to the Spanish colonies in the Americas were produced in Europe and in England. In addition, these countries supplied about 80 percent of the goods sold in Spain itself at this time. Spain paid for these foreign-made goods in colonial gold and silver. Through such trade, the nation's supplies of these precious metals decreased.

Political Issues Finally, the Spanish monarchs used their newfound wealth to finance large armies and navies, which then became involved in costly and devastating European wars. The most serious defeat was the English victory over the Spanish Armada in 1588. A Spanish fleet of about 130 ships had been sent to invade England but was destroyed. By the first half of the seventeenth century, other European countries had begun to challenge Spain in the Americas, and Spain was powerless to stop them.

See also: Aztec Empire; Columbus, Christopher; De Soto, Hernando; *The Diversity of Native America* in the Viewpoints section; Inca Empire; Mercantilism; Native Americans; Spain.

FURTHER READING
Elliot, J.H. *Imperial Spain*. New York: Penguin, 2002.
Parker, Geoffrey. *The Grand Strategy of Philip II*. New Haven, Conn.: Yale University Press, 2000.

New Sweden

Located on the Delaware River, a **colony** settled by Sweden. New Sweden covered parts of what are today Delaware, Maryland, Pennsylvania, and New Jersey.

In 1637, **stockholders** from Sweden, the Netherlands, and some German states formed the New Sweden Company. The purpose of the company was to trade for furs and tobacco in North America. The company's first expedition sailed from Sweden in late 1637 under the command of Peter Minuit. Well experienced, Minuit had been the governor of the Dutch colony of New Netherland from 1626 to 1631.

SETTLING NEW SWEDEN

In March 1638, the ships reached Delaware Bay, and the settlers began to build a fort at the site of present-day Wilmington, Delaware. They named it Fort Christina, in honor of Sweden's 12-year-old queen. Fort Christina was the first lasting European settlement in the Delaware Valley.

During the next 17 years, 11 ships and about 600 Swedes and Finns reached New Sweden. The colony eventually was made up of many farms and small settlements along both banks of the Delaware River.

New Sweden reached its height during the governorship of Johan Printz, who served from 1643 to 1653. He expanded the colony northward from Fort Christina along both sides of the Delaware River. Printz also improved the colony's military and economic position by building Fort Elfsborg, near present-day Salem on the New Jersey side of the river, to prevent English and Dutch ships from sailing up the Delaware. In general, the Swedish and Finnish **colonists**

N

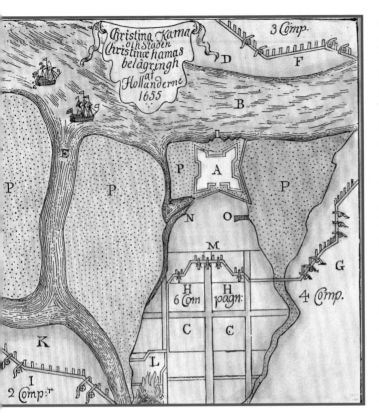

Built in 1638, Fort Christina was the first Swedish settlement in North America and the first permanent settlement in the Delaware Valley. In 1655, however, Dutch colonists from New Amsterdam to the north planned a siege of Fort Christina, as shown above, and the fort fell to the Dutch.

challenged the Dutch presence in the colony by seizing Fort Casimir, at the site of present-day New Castle, Delaware. With no gunpowder, Fort Casimir surrendered without a shot and was renamed Fort Trinity.

THE FALL OF NEW SWEDEN

Peter Stuyvesant was governor of the Dutch colony of New Netherland, which was located to the north of New Sweden. In the summer of 1655, seven armed Dutch ships and 317 Dutch soldiers appeared on the Delaware River. Realizing that resistance would be useless, the vastly outnumbered Swedes surrendered Fort Trinity. Governor Rising surrendered Fort Christina two weeks later.

Swedish rule over New Sweden was at an end. Stuyvesant, however, permitted the Swedish and Finnish colonists a great deal of **autonomy.** They were allowed to maintain their own **militia,** their religion, a court, and landholdings. They also were permitted to continue trading with the Indians. This degree of self-rule continued until 1681, when the Englishman William Penn received his charter from the English king for the lands that became the colonies of Pennsylvania and Delaware.

lived peacefully with their Dutch and Lenni Lenape neighbors.

Governor Printz's oppressive rule of the colony caused many of the settlers to become dissatisfied, however. Some of the settlers circulated a petition calling for reform within the colony, but the governor branded it a mutiny. In time, the petition did lead to the governor's return to Sweden, however.

In 1654, the colony's last governor, Johan Rising, succeeded Printz. Soon after arriving in New Sweden, Rising

See also: New Netherland; Thirteen Colonies; William Penn's Charter, in the "Viewpoints" section.

FURTHER READING
Taylor, Alan. *American Colonies: The Settling of North America.* New York: Penguin, 2006.

P–R

Plymouth Company

Founded in 1606 by England's King James I (r. 1603–1625) to establish profitable settlements on the eastern coast of North America, Plymouth Company was a **joint-stock company.**

The company's **shareholders** were merchants from Plymouth, Bristol, and Exeter in England. The Plymouth Company established the Popham colony on the coast of what is today Maine in 1607 but soon abandoned it.

In 1620, the Plymouth Company was reorganized under a new charter as the Plymouth Council for New England. In this charter, the company was given rights of settlement in the area now designated as New England. This vast area was previously part of the Virginia Colony, north of the 40th **parallel** of latitude in what is today central New Jersey. The land called New England extended north to the 48th parallel, thus including all of present-day New Brunswick and Nova Scotia in Canada. The new charter also established colonial rights of the company "from sea to sea."

PLYMOUTH COMPANY

Unlike the original Plymouth Company, the new Plymouth Council was successful. The first settlement in the area owned by the council was the Plymouth Colony in present-day Plymouth, Massachusetts. After the success of the Plymouth settlement, however, much of the rest of the company's land was given away in further grants to other colonial ventures.

After reaching the tip of Cape Cod, in what is today Massachusetts, the *Mayflower* sailed west to the area of today's Plymouth Harbor. This nineteenth century engraving shows John Alden, Mary Chilton, and other Pilgrims at Plymouth Rock in 1620.

P–R

Among the grants were that given to the Massachusetts Bay Company in 1628 and the grant of the Province of Maine to Sir Ferdinando Gorges and John Mason in 1622.

The Pilgrims who established Plymouth Colony had been granted permission by the London Company to settle near the mouth of the Hudson River, in the area of present-day New York City. Because the Pilgrims sailed too far north, and winter was approaching, they settled farther north, in Cape Cod Bay. The colony obtained land rights from the Plymouth Council in 1621 and 1630, but the Pilgrim colony was governed independently from the council, under the Pilgrim's own Mayflower Compact.

See also: England; London Company; *Mayflower*, The; Mayflower Compact; New England; Thirteen Colonies.

FURTHER READING
Deetz, James, and Patricia Scott Deetz. *The Times of Their Lives: Life, Love, and Death in Plymouth Colony.* New York: Anchor, 2001.

Portugal

Small European nation on the **Iberian Peninsula** that was responsible for the development of many innovations that led to the finding of a new route to Asia. Ultimately, these developments also led to the discovery and eventual colonization of the American continents.

The Europeans' voyages of exploration would not have been possible without changes in technology that took place during the **Renaissance**— a time of great change in Europe in manners of thinking and learning, the arts, and literature. In Portugal, a solid knowledge of sailing was combined with new ideas about technology and geography to provide a foundation for exploration. One person in particular, Prince Henry the Navigator, (1394–1460) was responsible for turning the Portuguese toward uncharted seas.

PRINCE HENRY THE NAVIGATOR
Prince Henry was the third son of the king of Portugal. He became interested in establishing trade with Africa around 1415. In Morocco, on Africa's northwest coast, Prince Henry had learned of gold routes across the Sahara, the vast desert of North Africa. To take advantage of these routes and to find a sea route to India and the lands of the spice trade, Prince Henry set up a navigation school at the city of Sagres in southwestern Portugal. Prince Henry also wanted to spread Christianity to Africa and India.

At the school, Henry brought together mathematicians, astronomers, and mapmakers. He wanted them to expand European navigational knowledge, to provide information about wind and sea currents, and to make the most up-to-date maps and charts.

Before the technological developments made by Prince Henry and the scholars at Sagres, sailors used instruments such as the magnetic compass to navigate when out of sight of land. Indeed, this compass was a sailor's most important tool for navigation. Slowly, European sailors also had begun to use an instrument called an astrolabe to find the height of the sun or the North Star above the horizon; this was the way to determine latitude. Distances were measured by very crude methods.

SAILING EXPEDITIONS

Between 1420 and 1450, using new navigational methods and better ships, Portuguese crews explored the Madeira Islands and the Azores in the eastern Atlantic Ocean. In the 1440s, the first cargo from Africa reached Portugal. Soon, trade in gold, ivory, pepper, and, sadly, slaves thrived.

In 1473, Portuguese sailors crossed the **equator.** Ten years later, they explored the mouth of the Congo River, on Africa's west coast. In 1488, Bartholomeu Diaz reached the southernmost point of Africa—the Cape of Good Hope. An all-water route to the Indian Ocean was found by Vasco da Gama, who sailed around Africa in 1497–1498.

See also: Da Gama, Vasco; New Spain; Spain.

FURTHER READING
Koestler-Grack, Rachel A. *Vasco da Gama and the Sea Route to India.* New York: Chelsea House, 2005.
Newitt, Malyn. *A History of Portuguese Overseas Expansion.* New York: Routledge, 2005.
Russell, Peter. *Prince Henry 'the Navigator': A Life.* New Haven, Conn.: Yale University Press, 2000.

Proclamation of 1763

Order issued by King George III (r. 1760–1820) that forbade English **colonists** from settling west of the Appalachian Mountains. After British regular troops and English colonial militias soundly defeated the French in the French and Indian War (1754–1763), the settlers of the thirteen British **colonies** eagerly looked forward to moving west into the region known as the Ohio River Valley.

As a result of the Treaty of Paris of 1763, which ended the French and Indian War, the British acquired almost all French lands in North America. The British set about to organize the lands; they established the boundaries of the new province of Quebec in Canada and of East Florida and West Florida to the south. On October 7, 1763, however, shortly after the treaty was signed, King George III issued the Proclamation of 1763.

The king made the proclamation for several reasons. First, several Indian groups, under the leadership of Chief Pontiac, were unhappy with the way the British treated them. Although the French had traded with the Indians, the British treated them as conquered peoples. In 1763, Pontiac and his followers attacked British forts and settlements in the Ohio River Valley, in an attempt to force the British out of the area.

Because the proclamation was designed to keep more settlers from entering the Ohio River Valley region, the king hoped it would help bring peace. Peace also would mean that fewer British soldiers would need to be stationed in the vast region. The cost of maintaining Britain's overseas empire would be less.

The king and his advisers had another economic motive, as well. Colonists who went far into the interior of the Ohio River Valley to settle would not be able to trade with Britain. In addition, because Britain was in difficult

P– R

financial straits at the time, the government planned to tax the colonists. It would be difficult for tax collectors to reach settlers in the far west. Overall, the distant settlements would be of little value to the British treasury.

COLONIAL REACTION

The Proclamation of 1763 did improve Britain's relations with the Ohio Valley Indians, but it greatly upset the colonists. From the colonists' point of view, one of the major reasons the French and Indian War was fought was to give English colonists access to land in the Ohio River Valley. The king's proclamation denied colonists this economic opportunity, and many colonists became convinced that England failed to understand colonists' needs.

The proclamation did not prevent the colonists from moving into the Ohio River Valley, however. Almost immediately after the French and Indian War, settlers began to move west. These settlers included many poor families from east of the Appalachians who sought a better life. Land **speculators**—men who wanted to buy land and then resell it at a profit—voiced strong objections to the crown. The Proclamation of 1763 was one factor that helped to separate the colonists from Britain in the years before the American Revolution (1775–1783). The proclamation remained in effect until 1776, when the American colonies declared their independence from England.

See also: Appalachian Mountains; French and Indian War; New France; Quebec; Thirteen Colonies.

Puritans

See Thirteen Colonies; Tobacco.

Quakers

See Thirteen Colonies.

Quebec

First permanent French settlement in North America. The first explorer to sail for the New World under the flag of France was Giovanni da Verrazano. In 1523 and 1524, he sailed along the coast of North America as far south as the Carolinas and as far north as Newfoundland in what is today Canada.

The next explorer the French king sent to America was Jacques Cartier. He explored the Gulf of St. Lawrence in 1534 and claimed the land around it for France. On a second voyage the following year, Cartier sailed up the St. Lawrence River as far as the site of present-day Montreal. In 1541, Cartier made yet another voyage, this time to set up a French settlement. The little colony, however, did not last.

More than a half-century passed before Samuel de Champlain led another group of settlers to the land that Cartier named Canada. On July 3, 1608, Champlain founded Quebec, the first lasting French settlement in the Americas. Champlain and his group erected a wooden building that served as a residence, a fort, and a storage place for the food and furs he traded. Cannons; a palisade, or fence, of wood stakes; a moat; and a drawbridge protected the entrance.

By 1609, Indians were visiting the little settlement regularly to trade furs for European goods. Later, in about 1615, Quebec also became a starting

The French in Quebec

French settlement of Quebec began in 1608, making it the oldest French city in North America. After the French and Indian War (1754–1763), the Treaty of Paris of 1763 formally transferred the French colony of Canada—including Quebec—to Great Britain. In 1774, fearful that the French-speaking population of Quebec would side with the inhabitants of the increasingly rebellious thirteen colonies to the south, the British Parliament passed the Quebec Act. The act recognized French law, the Catholic religion, and the French language in the colony. Up to that time, under British rule, Catholics had been excluded from public office, and the recruitment of priests had been forbidden. The act also restored the Ohio Valley to Quebec and reserved the territory for the fur trade.

French culture and traditions continued to thrive in Quebec. In 1867, the British Parliament passed the British North America Act, which established the Canadian Confederation. The provinces of New Brunswick and Nova Scotia joined English-speaking Ontario and French-dominated Quebec in the new Dominion of Canada. Although it was self-governing, the dominion was a part of the British Empire and recognized the British monarch as its ruler.

Through the years, many members of the French minority within Canada have resented the dominance of the English. This has been true even though the country is officially bilingual. In the 1970s and 1980s, many French in Quebec called for greater **autonomy** within Canada. Some called for Quebec to **secede** from Canada and become an independent nation.

In 1980, a referendum, or vote, was held on the question of Quebec's independence. Sixty percent of the voters in Quebec rejected the referendum. In 1995, another vote on the question was held. This time, voters defeated the referendum more narrowly, 50.6 percent to 49.4 percent. Today, Quebec remains a distinct society within Canada, and the question of independence for Quebec may come up for a vote yet again.

---

point for the Jesuit missionaries who worked to convert the Indians to Christianity. Despite the settlement's success as a trading post, however, Quebec still had only 72 inhabitants 20 years after its founding.

SLOW SETTLEMENT

Slowly, more settlers began to arrive in the Quebec area. The land was divided into *seigniories,* or landholdings, that extended inland in parallel strips from the St. Lawrence River, which served as the main means of transportation. In time, the seigniories covered the entire area of the modern-day city of Quebec.

Despite the ongoing threat from the Iroquois, who were bitter enemies of the French, most settlers preferred life in the countryside to that in the town. Owning land gave settlers a means of **subsistence** and something to pass down to their children. By about 1663, about 550 people were living in Quebec and 1,400 had settled in the surrounding countryside.

Quebec officially became the capital of New France in 1663. The city served as the seat of government as well as an administrative, judicial, and business center. The city also played an important role in religious affairs. The Quebec Seminary trained new priests for the colony, and in 1674, the city became home to a bishop's palace. From Quebec, French **missionaries** were sent throughout New France.

THE FALL OF QUEBEC

In 1754, warfare broke out between the French and the British in North America. At first, most of the fighting took place in the Ohio River Valley. Over the next three years, the French, lead by General Louis Joseph Montcalm, defeated the British in numerous battles. It seemed certain that the French would win.

In 1758, however, the British, under the leadership of Prime Minister William Pitt, rallied. Pitt sent more soldiers and supplies for the war effort. He also enlarged the size of the British Navy. Finally, Pitt sent new military leaders to direct the fighting— General James Wolfe and General Jeffrey Amherst.

In 1758, Amherst's army defeated the French at Louisbourg, a fort on the coast of Canada. This victory opened the St. Lawrence River to the British Navy. The following year, 250 British ships, carrying about 8,500 soldiers and twice as many sailors, sailed up the St. Lawrence and anchored off Quebec. General James Wolfe led this mighty British force, and his goal was to capture Quebec.

Quebec was difficult to attack, however, because of its location at the edge of steep cliffs. Below the cliffs, the swiftly flowing St. Lawrence River made landing dangerous for both ships and men. Wolfe's men spent several months searching the area to find a safe place to land. Finally, in September 1759, Wolfe located a landing place. He spotted some women washing clothes on the riverbank below Quebec and watched them as they took a hidden trail up to the city.

During the night of September 12–13, 1759, Wolfe led his men up the trail. By early that morning, about 4,000 British troops were in place for battle with the French. The British occupied the Plains of Abraham on the plateau above the cliffs and won a decisive victory over the French forces. Both Wolfe and Montcalm were killed during the fierce fighting. Five days later, the capital of New France surrendered.

Fighting continued elsewhere in Canada. The city of Montreal surrendered in 1760. With the Treaty of Paris of 1763, France lost almost all of its colonial possessions in North America. The former capital of New France became the capital of the British province of Quebec.

See also: Champlain, Samuel de; French and Indian War; New France; *The Opening of the Fur Trade* in the "Viewpoints" section.

FURTHER READING
Carroll, Joy. *Wolfe and Montcalm: Their Lives, Their Times, and the Fate of a Continent.* Richmond, Hill, On.: Firefly, 2004.
Hibbert, Christopher. *Wolfe at Quebec: The Man Who Won the French and Indian War.* Lanham, Md.: Cooper Square Press, 1999.

Roanoke, Lost Colony of

Failed settlement established in 1587 on the island of Roanoke, off the coast of what is today North Carolina. In 1578, an English scholar and soldier, Sir Humphrey Gilbert, asked Queen Elizabeth I (r. 1558–1603) for permission to renew the search for a sea route to Asia. He also requested a **charter** to set up a **colony.**

Using his own money, Gilbert outfitted an expedition of five ships, which reached Newfoundland in 1583. Gilbert explored the area, and, like John Cabot before him, claimed the land for England. Gilbert did not, however, find the fabled **Northwest Passage.** After one of the ships was lost at sea, the would-be **colonists** convinced Gilbert that they wanted to return home to England. On the return voyage, the ship carrying Gilbert sank, and he drowned.

The charter that Elizabeth I gave to Gilbert was inherited by his half-brother, Sir Walter Raleigh. Raleigh, well-known and well-educated, was a favorite of the queen. He was interested in exploration, and he was willing to spend his own money to help establish an empire for England.

In 1584, Raleigh sent two ships to explore the shores of North America. After they reached the area of what is today North Carolina, the ships sailed as far south as Spanish Florida. The ships returned to England, and their captains praised the new lands, which Raleigh named Virginia in honor of Queen Elizabeth, England's never-married Virgin Queen.

In 1585, an expedition of about 100 men was sent to Virginia, and a colony was set up on Roanoke Island. Shortages of food and supplies and threats from hostile Indians led the men to abandon the colony, however. When Sir Francis Drake's fleet stopped at Roanoke in 1586, after having raided Spanish ships in the West Indies, the Roanoke group eagerly accepted Drake's offer to take them back to England.

THE LOST COLONY

Despite this setback, Raleigh continued his efforts to set up a successful colony in the Americas. An expedition of three ships left England for Virginia in 1587. Under the leadership of John White, about 100 men, women, and children settled on Roanoke Island. Among the settlers at Roanoke were White's daughter and her husband. They became the parents of Virginia Dare, the first English child born in North America. After four months, John White returned to England to get supplies. Because of the ongoing war between Spain and England, however, supply ships could not be sent for several years.

Raleigh finally arranged for the colony to be resupplied in 1590. When the ships, under the command of John White, finally arrived at Roanoke, however, there was no trace of any of the colonists. The only clue to the missing people was the word *CROATOAN* carved on a tree. Croatoan was the name of an island to the southwest of Roanoke.

White organized a search party to find the colonists but was unsuccessful. Several theories have been suggested to explain the disappearance of the colonists, but their fate remains a mystery.

See also: Drake, Sir Francis; England; Jamestown, Virginia; Thirteen Colonies.

FURTHER READING

Kupperman, Karen O. *Roanoke: The Abandoned Colony.* Lanham, Md.: Rowman & Littlefield, 2007.

Miller, Lee. *Mystery of the Lost Colony.* New York: Scholastic, 2007.

Russia

Located in Eastern Europe and Northern Asia, nation that once had claims to the northwestern part of North America. Russia made its first claims to North America in the early 1700s.

VITUS BERING'S EXPEDITIONS

Under orders from Czar Peter the Great (r. 1682–1725), the Danish explorer Vitus Bering left St. Petersburg, Russia in early 1725, leading an expedition that traveled eastward across Siberia. The group set up a base on the Kamchatka Peninsula, on Russia's Pacific coast, and built ships that were designed to explore the sea. In 1728, Bering sailed north through the strait that now bears his name, proving that America and Asia were separate continents. The expedition finally returned to St. Petersburg in 1730.

In 1733, the Russian government under Empress Anna (r. 1730–1740) commissioned Bering for another expedition. Known as The Great Nordic Expedition, this huge enterprise was a quest to map the Russian-Siberian coast and the western coast of America as far south as Mexico. Bering and his group reached Kamchatka in 1740,

having spent the first years of their journey exploring northern Siberia.

In 1741, the expedition set out by sea from the settlement of Okhotsk, rounded the Kamchatka Peninsula, and founded the town of Petropavlovsk on the peninsula's east coast. The group then sailed eastward to America. Bering sighted the St. Elias Mountains on the northern coast of the Gulf of Alaska on July 16. Bad weather, however, forced the expedition to return to Kamchatka. On the return trip, Bering sailed past Alaska's Kodiak Island and discovered some of the Aleutian Islands.

As the expedition sailed home, Bering became ill with **scurvy,** a disease caused by a lack of vitamin C, and was too sick to command his ships. With the harsh northern winter approaching, the members of the expedition took refuge on an uninhabited island in the Commander Islands, just east of Kamchatka. The sick and weary explorers mistook the islands for the Kamchatka coast. The men spent the winter living in driftwood huts built into the sand. On December 19, 1741, Bering died on the island that later came to bear his name. Nearly half of his company also died. The few survivors finally reached Kamchatka in the summer of 1742.

THE RUSSIAN AMERICAN COMPANY

In 1799, Czar Paul I (r. 1796–1801) granted a **charter** to the Russian American Company. The charter gave the company a monopoly on trade in Russian America, which included the Aleutian Islands, Alaska, and Russian claims farther south along the North

American coast. Under the terms of the charter, one-third of all profits were to go to the czar.

Aleksandr Baranov, who governed Russian America between 1790 and 1818, built a permanent settlement in 1804 at Novo-Arkhangelsk, the site of present-day Sitka, Alaska. At first, the fur trade thrived. By the 1820s, however, the profits from the fur trade began to decline. High transportation costs kept the colony from ever becoming profitable. The Russian American Company also constructed forts to the south, along the coasts of what are today Alaska and California.

Fort Ross, on the California coast just north of present-day San Francisco, was the southernmost outpost of Russian America. It was established by Ivan Kuskov of the Russian American Company in 1812 and was a thriving settlement until 1841. At first, the company carried on a fur-trading business at Fort Ross, but the fort later concentrated on **agriculture** and small industry to supply the Alaskan settlements to the north.

By the early 1860s, Russia had decided to sell its American lands. In 1867, U.S. secretary of state William H. Seward negotiated a treaty for the purchase of Russian Alaska. The United States acquired Alaska for $7,200,000, a price of less than two cents per acre.

FURTHER READING

Black, Lydia T. *Russians in Alaska: 1732–1867.* Fairbanks: University of Alaska Press, 2004.

Frost, Orcutt. *Bering: The Russian Discovery of America.* New Haven, Conn.: Yale University Press, 2003.

S-V

Slavery and the Slave Trade

The capture and forced labor of Africans who were brought to work in the Americas. Between the sixteenth and the first half of the nineteenth centuries, about 12 to 15 million human beings were taken from their homes in West Africa and transported to the Caribbean Islands and the Americas, mostly to work on plantations.

Some Africans themselves dealt in slaves and sold their own people to European slave traders. In some cases, Africans were forced into slavery because of debt or for having committed a crime. In other cases, men and women were captured during wars between African nations.

THE ATLANTIC SLAVE TRADE

The Portuguese were the first Europeans to visit Africa south of the Sahara and the first to take slaves, beginning in about 1440. Most of these slaves were shipped to southern Portugal, where they worked chiefly as household servants. As Portugal's colonies in the Americas grew, however, laborers were needed to work on the huge sugarcane plantations of Brazil. In 1518, the first of thousands of slave ships tightly packed with human cargo crossed the Atlantic Ocean, bound for the Americas.

The slave trade became very profitable for the Portuguese, and other colonial European powers quickly became aware of this fact. Before long,

S–V

Spain, England, France, and the Netherlands began to compete for their share of slave-trade wealth. Over a period of about 300 years, slave traders made more than 50,000 voyages across the Atlantic, a 4,000-mile (6,437.38-kilometer) journey that took about three months. About 42 percent of the slaves ended up working on plantations in the Caribbean region. Another 38 percent went to Brazil. About 5 percent of the slaves were brought to North America.

THE MIDDLE PASSAGE

By all accounts, crossing the Atlantic was a nightmare for the enslaved Africans. The journey between Africa and the Americas became known as the Middle Passage. On the slave ships, the human cargo was kept below decks, where the air was stale and carried often deadly disease, and where there was barely room to move. People urinated and defecated where they lay, and many died of disease or despair.

Some people committed suicide by banging their heads against the floor, deliberately refusing to eat, or jumping overboard. Food, while plentiful, was of the poorest quality. It was served in buckets, which led to fights as terrified individuals struggled to get their share. Although the slave traders had an economic investment in keeping their unwilling passengers alive, at least 20 percent of the human cargo aboard the slave ships died before the ships reached the Americas.

In general, the European slavers did not capture the slaves themselves. The slave ships arrived at ports along the west coast of Africa, in places such as Guinea and the Gold Coast, in present-day Ghana. In these ports, African traders who had captured people in the interior of the continent would sell them to the Europeans. Many Africans grew rich, not only by selling slaves but also by trading in the supplies that were needed for the long sea journeys across the Atlantic.

When Europeans later banned the slave trade, many African traders and some leaders became angry; they felt that their livelihoods were being taken away. Some African kings, however, recognized that their kingdoms were losing their strongest and best people to slavery. The king of Benin stopped trafficking in slaves in the early sixteenth century. King Afonso I (r. 1509–1542/3) of Kongo protested to the king of Portugal and to the pope that slavery was destroying his kingdom.

SLAVERY IN THE THIRTEEN COLONIES

In 1619, a Dutch ship carrying about 20 Africans landed in Jamestown, Virginia. These first Africans to arrive in Jamestown were treated as **indentured servants** by the English **colonists.** In Virginia, the change of Africans' status from indentured servants to slaves occurred gradually. There were no laws regarding slavery early in the Virginia colony's history. By 1640, however, the Virginia courts had sentenced at least one black servant to slavery.

In 1654, John Casor, a black man, became the first legally recognized slave in the thirteen British North American colonies. A court in Northampton County, Virginia, ruled against Casor, declaring him property for life and stating that he was "owned" by the black colonist Anthony Johnson. Because Africans were not English citizens by birth, English law did not protect them. In 1662, a Hereditary Slavery law in Virginia declared that children of black mothers "shall be bond or free according to the condition of the mother."

The Virginia Slave codes of 1705 made the status of slaves brutally clear. As the codes noted,

If any slave resist his master. . . correcting such slave, and shall happen to be killed in such correction. . .the master shall be free of all punishment. . . as if such accident never happened.

During the colonial period, slavery was legal in all of the thirteen colonies. Slaves in the north worked mainly as household servants. As early as the 1630s, however, slaves in the southern colonies worked on farms and plantations, growing indigo, rice, and tobacco. (Cotton did not became a major crop until after the 1790s.) By 1720, about 65 percent of South Carolina's total population consisted of enslaved people.

Conditions of the Enslaved Slaves were sold as property and worked without reward for their masters. Masters might care for slaves as they did for any valuable property, but enslaved people were entirely subject to their masters' wishes. African slaves often were thought of as more desirable than free white servants. Africans could be identified more easily if they ran away. Many whites believed that blacks were "naturally suited" for labor and subservience.

The life of a slave was difficult. On large plantations, overseers were authorized to whip slaves if they thought such punishment was necessary. Both slaves and free blacks were regulated by laws called "slave codes" and had their movements monitored by slave patrols. These patrols often were allowed to punish escaped slaves as they saw fit and sometimes maimed or killed their victims.

Under the slave codes, a slave was not allowed to leave his or her master's property except when accompanied by a white person or when carrying a travel permit. In addition, large gatherings of slaves, except those supervised by an overseer, were not permitted. Slaves were forbidden to learn how to read and write. Anyone who broke any of the slave codes or other rules was severely punished.

In addition to physical abuse and murder, slaves were at constant risk of losing members of their families. Slaveholders could trade or sell slaves for profit, for punishment, or to pay financial debts. Untold numbers of slave families were wrenched apart in such transactions. Enslaved women often were abused by white male owners or overseers. In some households, the treatment of slaves varied with the slave's skin color. Darker-skinned slaves usually worked in the fields. Lighter-skinned house servants often had better clothing, food, and housing.

Rights of the Enslaved Because slaves were considered chattel—personal private property—they had no legal rights. Even the right to get married was denied to slaves. Many slaves

S–V

went through a form of marriage that was recognized by most slaveholders, however. Married slaves lived together and raised families. The fear that a family member might be sold placed great stress on slave families, however.

At first, slavery thrived in all thirteen British colonies but did so especially in the south, where slave labor was more profitable. At about the time of the American Revolution (1775–1783), many northern colonies began to **abolish** slavery. In the post-Revolution south, however, the demand for slaves increased in the 1790s, after Eli Whitney invented the cotton gin, a machine that quickly and easily removed the seeds from the cotton fiber. Slavery remained legal in the United States until the Thirteenth Amendment was added to the Constitution in 1865.

ENDING THE SLAVE TRADE
Several factors contributed to the ending of the slave trade. The British were the first to outlaw the practice; they put an end to slave trading in 1807 and banned the ownership of slaves in 1834. With the efforts of British **abolitionists** such as Granville Sharp and William Wilberforce, the **industrial revolution** itself contributed to the end of slavery because industrial processes and factories, unlike plantations, worked better with free labor. Furthermore, because the British had lost their American colonies in 1783, they no longer had a captive market for slaves.

The French Revolution, which began in 1789, emphasized liberty and equality, and further strengthened the idea that slavery and slave trading were morally wrong. The French outlawed slave trading in 1818, and Spain did so in 1820. Portugal outlawed the slave trade in 1830, but trading actually continued through the 1850s. The Dutch outlawed the slave trade in 1863. By 1888, when slavery ended in Brazil, slavery was abolished throughout the Americas. Despite this, it is estimated that several hundred thousand people work under slavelike conditions today, mainly on sugar plantations in Brazil and the Dominican Republic.

See also: England; Jamestown, Virginia; Native Americans; Netherlands; Portugal; Thirteen Colonies.

FURTHER READING
Kamma, Anna. *If You Lived When There Was Slavery in America.* New York: Scholastic, 2004.
Lovejoy, Paul E. *Transformations in Slavery: A History of Slaves in Africa.* Cambridge: Cambridge University Press, 2000.
Smallwood, Stephanie E. *Saltwater Slavery: A Middle Passage from Africa to American Diaspora.* Cambridge, Mass.: Harvard University Press, 2007.
Taylor, Yuval. *Growing Up in Slavery: Stories of Young Slaves as Told By Themselves.* Chicago: Lawrence Hill, 2007.

Smith, John (1580–1631)

Explorer, writer, **colonist,** and soldier who saved the Jamestown settlement. Smith is now regarded as the one who kept the English colonists alive. In his own time, however, he was seen as an arrogant and combative braggart.

Smith was born in 1580 in Willoughby, near Lincolnshire, England. As a child, he attended King Edward VI Grammar School in Louth, approximately 15 miles (24 kilometers) from his home. When Smith's father died in 1596, John left home to become a soldier and sailor.

His introduction to war was with a company of English soldiers sent to fight against the Spaniards in support of Dutch independence. He also fought as a **mercenary** for King Henry IV (r. 1589–1610) of France. In 1600, Smith joined a regiment and fought against the Ottoman Turks in the Long War, a 13-year conflict between the Ottomans and the Austrians.

Smith proved to be an inventive military man. He freed the town of Limbach from Turkish control by using a line of string and gunpowder to copy the look of musket fire at night. The Turks were drawn to the western end of the town by Smith's display as the Austrians moved in from the east. For this action, Smith was promoted to captain. Later, to free a different town, Smith built savagely effective bombs by filling clay pots with powder and covering them with tar, brimstone, turpentine, and musket balls. These were set on fire and hurled over the city walls.

Smith continued to fight for the Austrians under Mihai Viteazul, or Michael the Brave, who united Transylvania, Moldovia, and Wallachia, in what is today Romania. After Michael's assassination, Smith joined Transylvanian Prince Sigismund Báthory's army. During this time, Smith was knighted for killing three Turks in duels.

In 1602, Smith was badly wounded in battle, captured, and sold as a slave. He was bought by a Turk and sent to Constantinople, the capital of the Ottoman Empire. Smith was beaten regularly and had little to eat. He escaped when his master came out to the fields where Smith was threshing wheat. Because his master was going to beat him again, Smith hit him on the head with the threshing bat and killed him. Smith then hid the body, stole the man's clothes, and rode north into Russia, the closest Christian country, where he hoped to find help. A year later, in 1604, John Smith finally made it back to England.

At the time of Smith's return, England was in a rush to colonize the Americas. Smith joined the Virginia Company, whose three ships sailed to found an American colony on December 20, 1606. At some point before the fleet reached the Canary Islands, off the coast of Africa, Smith was accused of plotting mutiny and planning to make himself king of Virginia.

This accusation probably originated in a dispute between Edward Maria Wingfield, an English gentleman of high rank, and Smith, who refused to show what Wingfield considered proper respect to one of his betters. Wingfield and his allies intended to hang Smith, the first official prisoner in English America. Captain Christopher Newport, the highest-ranking member of the fleet, stopped the execution, however.

BATTLE FOR SURVIVAL AT JAMESTOWN

In May 1607, the colonists arrived in Virginia and established the settlement of Jamestown, named in honor of King James I (r. 1603–1625). The conditions at Jamestown were difficult. The Powhatan attacked the new

S–V

colony two weeks after it was founded. In addition, the Jamestown colonists were starved for food and suffered from disease. Because the journey from England had taken longer than expected, the colonists had eaten much of their food stored and had arrived too late to plant crops. To make conditions worse, class disputes continued to be a problem. The gentlemen refused to do the work of laborers.

The only way to get food was to trade with the Powhatan. Smith traded hatchets and other goods for bushels of corn. Although reports are mixed as to whether Smith traded peacefully or by using force, it is clear that he saved the Jamestown colony from starvation.

The Legend of Pocahontas The most famous incident in John Smith's career was his encounter with the local Indians. He had taken a party of men out to search for food along the Chickahominy River. The group was ambushed, and two men were killed. The rest were taken to Chief Wahunsunacock, often referred to as Powhatan. According to Smith's account, the chief had two large rocks placed before him. Smith's captors wrestled him over to the stones, placed his head down on them, and readied their clubs. Smith then says that "Pocahontas the King's dearest daughter, when no entreaty would prevail, got his head in her arms, and laid her own upon his to save him from death."

This one line has been spun into a romantic legend. The incident is mentioned in only one of Smith's books, 15 years after it supposedly happened.

While many interpreters have made the story out to be a romantic one, some scholars believe that Powhatan was acting out a ritual that brought Smith into his tribe, essentially turning the Englishman into a subordinate. Whether or not it is true that Pocahontas saved Smith's life, Smith believed that she did. What is certain is that Pocahontas continued to help him and the Jamestown colony. She brought them warning of an impending attack and provided food when they were starving.

PRESIDENT OF THE COLONY

In 1608, John Smith was elected president of the Jamestown colony and quickly started to make improvements. He had a well dug and houses built. He sent out regular fishing trips and made sure that crops were planted. He is quoted as having said, "that he that will not work shall not eat (except by sickness he be disabled) for the labors of thirty or forty honest and industrious men shall not be consumed to maintain an hundred and fifty idle loiterers."

This strict rule—that everyone who eats must also work—is credited with saving the Jamestown settlement. More settlers soon arrived from England, however, and this made the food shortage worse. Smith was forced to steal supplies from native villages that would not trade.

These raids eventually ended the friendship between Smith and Powhatan, and the English and the Indians began to attack one another in force. Following one conflict, as Smith headed back to Jamestown by boat, a spark ignited a powder bag on his arm, and he was badly burned. In October of 1609, Smith left for England to get medical treatment for his injury and to face charges that the other councilors at Jamestown had filed against him. None of the charges ever were proved.

NEW ENGLAND

Although he never returned to Virginia, John Smith returned to North America once more. In 1614, he explored the coasts of Maine and Massachusetts Bay. He named this area "New England." Smith fished the local waters and returned to England, determined to find funding for a colony of his own. In 1615, he sailed again to New England, only to be taken prisoner by French **privateers;** his own people sailed away while he was onboard a French vessel. When the French ship sank in a storm, Smith escaped in a small boat. He returned to England and pressed charges against the men who had left him with the French. Smith never reached New England again. He spent the rest of his life in England, writing about his adventures. He died in 1631 at the age of 51.

See also: England; Jamestown, Virginia; Native Americans; New England.

FURTHER READING

Hoobler, Dorothy, and Thomas Hoobler. *Captain John Smith: Jamestown and the Birth of the American Dream.* Hoboken, N.J.: John Wiley & Sons, 2006.

Spain

Located on the **Iberian Peninsula;** European nation that once ruled a rich, worldwide empire. In the late 1400s, the unification of the kingdoms of Aragon, Castile, León, and Navarre under King Ferdinand (r. 1479–1516) and Queen Isabella (r. 1474–1504) laid the basis for modern Spain and the Spanish empire.

By the end of the sixteenth century, Spain had become Europe's leading power. Reinforced by trade and wealth from its colonial possessions, Spain retained this position through the seventeenth century.

Throughout the 1500s and 1600s, the Spanish empire expanded to include most of South America, Central America, Mexico, the southern and western parts of what is today the United States, the Philippines, and the western Pacific island of Guam. Later, through its ruling **Habsburg Dynasty,** Spain controlled southern Italy, the island of Sicily, and parts of present-day Belgium, Luxembourg, and the Netherlands.

EXPLORATIONS AND CLAIMS

In 1492, after Spanish armies drove the Moors, Muslims who lived in Spain, from Granada in southern Spain, Ferdinand and Isabella sent Christopher Columbus, an Italian sea captain from Genoa, westward in the hope of finding the riches of Asia. Spain was seeking to counter the explorations and successes of its rival Portugal, whose explorers had been sailing around Africa. Instead of discovering an all-water route to Asia, however, Columbus found the Americas. Thus began the Spanish colonization of the North and South American continents and the islands of the Caribbean.

Spain's claim to these lands was recognized by the pope in 1493 and by the Treaty of Tordesillas of 1494.

Under this treaty, the globe was divided into two **hemispheres,** with a line drawn between the Spanish and Portuguese claims. These actions gave Spain exclusive rights to establish colonies in all of the Americas except Brazil, which was allotted to Portugal.

Almost immediately after Columbus's first voyage, Spain started to send **colonists** to the Americas. After the settlement of the island of Hispaniola—present-day Haiti and the Dominican Republic—in the early 1500s, some of the colonists began looking for other lands in which to begin new outposts. From Hispaniola, Juan Ponce de León conquered the island of Puerto Rico and then explored Florida. Diego Velázquez claimed Cuba. The first Spanish settlement on the American mainland was Darién, in Panama. It was established by Vasco Nuñez de Balboa in 1512.

In 1513, Balboa crossed the Isthmus of Panama and led the first European expedition to see the Pacific Ocean. Balboa, claimed the Pacific Ocean and all the lands touching it for the Spanish crown.

After Columbus's four voyages, the Spanish exploration of the Americas was led by a series of **conquistadors**—conquerors who searched for gold and other riches for themselves, as well as for Spain. These conquistador-led Spanish forces exploited the hatreds and rivalries that existed among local peoples. In this way, the Spanish often found willing **allies** for their fights against powerful empires such as those of the Aztec and the Inca.

Sadly, the Spanish conquest also was helped by the spread of diseases such as smallpox. Smallpox was common in Europe but was unknown in the Americas. Such illnesses spread quickly through populations with no inbred resistance and resulted in large numbers of deaths among the native inhabitants.

Hernán Cortés was one of the most successful conquistadors. With a relatively small Spanish force and hundreds of Indian allies, he toppled the mighty Aztec empire between 1519 and 1522. What is today Mexico became a part of the vast Spanish empire. The area later became known as New Spain.

Another important conquistador was Francisco Pizarro. In 1532, he conquered the vast Inca empire in South America. The Inca lands later became the **vice-royalty** of Peru. After the conquest of Mexico, rumors of "golden cities" spread through the Spanish colonies. Several expeditions were sent out in search of these mythical cities, but none of the explorers found their golden goal.

DECLINE

During the last half of the sixteenth century and through the seventeenth century, Spain was challenged from all sides. Barbary pirates who sailed under the protection of the powerful Ottoman Empire disrupted shipping with slave raids in Mediterranean coastal areas. At the same time, in Italy and elsewhere, Spain often was at war with France. In addition, Spain was dragged into a series of religious wars that stemmed from the **Protestant Reformation** and the Catholic **Counter-Reformation.** As a result, the country was pulled into military efforts across Europe and in the Mediterranean region.

During the second half of the seventeenth century, Spain went into a slow decline, even as it maintained its vast overseas empire. Most of Spain's colonies in the Americas gained independence in the early 1800s.

See also: Aztec Empire; Balboa, Vasco Nuñez de; Columbus, Christopher; De Soto, Hernando; Ferdinand and Isabella; Inca Empire; New Spain.

FURTHER READING
Alonso, Roberto Velesco, *et al. The Aztec Empire.* New York: Guggenheim Museum, 2004.
DiConsiglio, John. *Francisco Pizarro: Destroyer of the Inca Empire.* New York: Franklin Watts, 2008.
Doak, Robin S. *Christopher Columbus: Explorer of the New World.* Mankato, Minn.: Compass Point Press, 2005.
Elliot, J.H. *Imperial Spain, 1469–1716.* New York: Penguin, 2002.
Kamen, Henry. *Empire: How Spain Became a World Power, 1492–1763.* New York: HarperCollins, 2003.
Saunders, Nicholas J., and Tony Allan. The *Aztec Empire: Excavating the Past.* Portsmouth, N.H.: Heinemann Library, 2004.
Somerville, Barbara A. *Empire of the Inca.* New York: Facts On File, 2004.

Squanto (1585?–1622)

An Indian of the Patuxet tribe who lived in what is now Massachusetts and proved to be a valuable friend to the first settlers at Plymouth. Squanto also was known as Tisquantum. Squanto acted as a guide and interpreter for the first English settlers, helping them to explore and survive in the new lands. In 1621, he taught the starving Pilgrims about basic fishing and farming. A year later, Squanto became ill and died.

CAPTURE

In 1605, the English seafarer George Weymouth led an expedition to North America to assess the natural resources of the area. He explored the eastern coast of what is today Canada and New England. He sailed down the coast of Maine to Massachusetts, where he landed. He then decided to bring some of the local inhabitants back with him to England. Weymouth and his men kidnapped five Indians, one of whom was Squanto, and brought them aboard his ship.

In England, Squanto lived with Sir Ferdinando Gorges, a shareholder in the Plymouth Company. Gorges taught Squanto basic English and then hired Squanto to be a guide and interpreter for his sea captains as they explored the New England coast.

Return to America In 1614, Squanto returned to America, where he helpd John Smith and Gorges's men map the New England coast. After Smith finished mapping the Cape Cod region, he left Thomas Hunt in charge of the expedition so that the English could continue to trade with the Indians. Smith then left the area. With Smith gone, Hunt tricked 27 local Indians into coming onboard his ship to trade. When the Indians were onboard, Hunt kidnapped them. Squanto, onboard to act as an interpreter, also was captured.

Trip to Spain Hunt sailed to Malaga, Spain, where he tried to sell his captives as slaves. Some local priests discovered what was happening,

Squanto was one of the native people who befriended the Pilgrims during their first year at Plymouth Colony. Squanto, who had been kidnapped and taken to Europe, spoke English well and easily communicated with the colonists. In this drawing, he shows Pilgrims how to plant corn.

he was recognized by Captain Thomas Dermer, who had worked for Ferdinando Gorges in the past.

Across the Atlantic Again Thomas Dermer brought Squanto back to England. After working out the details, Gorges organized a trip to send Dermer and Squanto to explore Newfoundland and restart trade with the Indians along the New England coast. At the end of the expedition, Squanto was told, he would be returned to his home among the Patuxet people.

Dermer and Squanto worked together to map the New England coast. In 1619, when they arrived at Squanto's village, they found that the entire Patuxet community had been killed by a plague two years earlier. Squanto was the only member of his tribe left alive. He moved in with a neighboring tribe that lived at Pokanoket, the home of the Wampanoag **sachem,** or chief, Massasoit.

however, and took the Indian captives from Hunt. The priests then began to teach the former captives the Christian faith.

Squanto lived with the priests for a while and then fled to England. There, he lived with John Slaney, a merchant. In 1618, Squanto boarded a ship headed for Newfoundland. When he arrived in Newfoundland, however,

HELPING THE PILGRIMS

In November 1620, about a year after Squanto was returned to his homeland, the Pilgrims arrived. The Pilgrims explored the surrounding region and decided, in late December, to settle at Plymouth. Two months after the settlement was established at Plymouth, Samoset, an Indian visiting from what is now Maine, walked into the middle of the community, still being built. He welcomed the Pilgrims in English. The Pilgrims were astounded.

After much talk and some trading of goods, Samoset left the settlement to tell the Wampanoag that the Pilgrims wanted to make peace. Massasoit, the chief, then sent Squanto as an interpreter.

On March 22, 1621, the Pilgrims met Squanto for the first time. On that day, Squanto negotiated a peace treaty between the Wampanoag and the Pilgrims. It stated that the Wampanoag and the Pilgrims would not harm each other. The treaty became a military alliance as well: If one group was attacked, the other would come to its aid.

Squanto lived the rest of his life in the Plymouth Colony. He befriended the Pilgrims, taught them how to use manure to fertilize their corn, showed them where to catch fish and eels, and acted as their interpreter. Without Squanto's help, most of the Pilgrims probably would have had starved to death. In November 1622, Squanto set out on a trading expedition to the Massachusetts Indians. During the trip, Squanto came down with a fever and died.

See also: New England; Plymouth Company; Smith, John; Thirteen Colonies.

FURTHER READING
Hirschfelder, Arlene B. *Squanto, 1585?–1622.* Mankato, Minn.: Blue Earth Books, 2003.

Stuyvesant, Peter

See New Netherland.

Thirteen Colonies

Cluster of English **colonies** that hugged the Atlantic Seaboard and eventually became the independent nation of the United States of America. Many of the thirteen colonies eventually became royal colonies, which were run by the English government, but they still maintained their own governors and colonial legislatures. The roots of today's American government are drawn from the experience of the thirteen colonies.

VIRGINIA

In 1606, King James I of England (r. 1603–1625) granted charters to two **joint-stock companies**—the Plymouth Company and the London Company—to develop trade and colonize parts of North America. In 1607, about 100 men and boys, financed by the London Company, founded Jamestown in Virginia. Jamestown, named after the English king, became England's first permanent colony in North America.

At first, the **colonists** at Jamestown were pleased with the "fair meadows and goodly tall trees, with fresh water running through the woods." They set up tents and then built rough huts, as well as a fort. Soon, however, sickness brought hunger and disaster. Before long, about half of the settlers had died.

Few of the Jamestown settlers knew anything about farming. Most of the colonists were interested in searching for gold or other riches,

S–V

rather than in planting crops. John Smith, one of the colony's leaders, forced some of the men to cut down trees and clear land to plant crops, even though the men were not used to such hard work. Times became worse when more colonists arrived without bringing enough fresh food. The winter of 1609–1610 became known as "the starving time." Only about 60 of the first 500 colonists survived.

The nearby Indians, led by a chief known as Powhatan, helped the tiny settlement survive the first winter. By bringing corn and meat to the settlers, the Indians kept them from starving.

When the settlers learned to grow their own food and hunt wild game, the colony took root. At first, the colony had nothing to send back to England to sell at a profit. After 1612, however, the settlers sent tobacco to England. The colonists had learned how to grow this **cash crop** from the Indians.

Government Jamestown was first governed by a colonial council, which was chosen by the London Company. Later, an all-powerful governor took the place of the council. In 1619, the London Company ordered the colonists to elect a lawmaking assembly. This first legislature, known as the House of Burgesses, met in Jamestown in August 1619. The 22 members came from 11 towns and plantations. This first meeting of the House of Burgesses marked the beginning of self-government in the English colonies.

Although **stockholders** in the London Company—later called the Virginia Company—hoped for profits, about the only returns they received were grants of land. The company itself failed, and in 1624, King James I canceled its charter. James I then made Virginia the first English royal colony and placed it under his direct control.

NEW ENGLAND COLONIES

Plymouth, in what is now Massachusetts, became the second English colony in the Americas and the first in the region known as New England. It was founded in 1620 by a group of English Separatists who believed in governing their own churches. They had separated, or broken away, from the Church of England. King James I, as the head of the English church, found these beliefs to be dangerous. If the Separatists could defy the Church of England, they might defy the government as well.

Many of these Separatists, who called themselves Pilgrims, were from the little English village of Scrooby. Persecuted in England, the Pilgrims first moved to the Netherlands. There, they could worship as they pleased, but they found life difficult. Jobs were hard to find. They also feared that their children were learning Dutch ways and customs and losing their Separatists beliefs.

In 1620, some of these Pilgrims returned to England and, with other **migrants,** sailed for America on a ship called the *Mayflower.* Merchants from the Virginia Company helped to finance the Pilgrims, and King James I, happy to see the religious dissenters leave, allowed them to sail to the Americas.

The Pilgrims had received permission to settle on land granted to the Virginia Company, but they were blown off course. They landed to the north of their intended destination, in an area assigned to the Plymouth Company. Because they landed in a region where there was no government, they agreed among themselves to make fair laws and to obey them. This agreement, known as the Mayflower Compact, gave the colony a form of self-government.

The Pilgrims landed on Cape Cod in Massachusetts in November 1620 and later moved to nearby Plymouth. Because no one interfered with their colony, the Pilgrims remained at Plymouth and eventually secured the title to the area. Plymouth remained a self-governing colony until 1691. In that year, King William III (r. 1689–1702) of England transferred political control of the colony to Massachusetts.

Massachusetts Bay Colony Another group in England wanted to simplify the ways of the Church of England. In their words, they wished to "purify" the church. These people became known as Puritans.

Puritan leaders in England organized the Massachusetts Bay Company and obtained the right from King James I to land in New England. Only Puritans who wanted to leave England could hold shares in the Massachusetts Bay Company. The shares gave them a right to vote in all elections held by the company. In this way, the Massachusetts Bay Company became the government of the new colony.

Settlements in the Massachusetts Bay Colony proved much more important than those around Plymouth. In 1630, John Winthrop, the governor of the company, and about 700 Puritans set sail across the Atlantic. They brought with them their livestock, farm tools, and furnishings. In the next decade, thousands of Puritans came to Massachusetts to worship as they pleased. From the start, the colony grew and prospered.

The Puritans in Massachusetts vowed "to build a city of God on earth." The "city" that they built, however, required complete agreement with the colony's religious leaders. Although persecuted themselves in England, the Puritans in Massachusetts persecuted anyone who did not follow their own strict religious beliefs.

Religious differences and a desire for better land caused some colonists to leave Massachusetts and settle elsewhere. As a result, three other New England colonies were established by 1638: Rhode Island, New Hampshire, and Connecticut.

Rhode Island Roger Williams came to Massachusetts in 1631 but soon got into trouble with the religious authorities. His liberal beliefs and views went against those of Governor Winthrop and other Puritan leaders. Because of his beliefs, Williams was banished from Massachusetts in 1635. Williams and some of his followers founded Providence, Rhode Island, in 1636. Other people fleeing the strict rule of Massachusetts soon joined Williams.

Anne Hutchinson was another colonist who questioned the authority of the Puritans in Massachusetts. She was banished from the colony because of her religious views and moved to Rhode Island in 1638. She and her followers established a settlement at the site of what is today

S–V

Portsmouth. In 1663, King Charles II (r. 1660–1685) granted Rhode Island a charter, which served as the basis for the colony's government. Rhode Island was the first English colony to allow religious freedom.

New Hampshire The Reverend John Wheelwright, a brother-in-law of Anne Hutchinson, was also banished from Massachusetts because of his liberal religious beliefs. In 1638, he established a settlement at Exeter, New Hampshire. Although King Charles I (r. 1625–1649) had granted New Hampshire to an adventurer named John Mason, settlements established at Exeter and throughout the New Hampshire region became the basis for the colony. New Hampshire became a royal colony in 1680.

Connecticut The Reverend Thomas Hooker was another colonist who disagreed with the strict rules of the Puritans in Massachusetts. Hooker also believed that people should have a greater voice in their own government. In 1636, he led his followers westward to the fertile Connecticut River Valley. Traveling along trails made by the Indians, these settlers brought cattle and supplies with them. They founded the town of Hartford. Soon, other settlers set up the towns of Windsor, Wethersfield, and New Haven.

Arriving in 1682, William Penn, the Quaker founder of Pennsylvania, is warmly greeted by fellow Quakers and Indians from the area. Penn's colony allowed people of all faiths to worship freely.

In 1639, the leaders of these towns drew up a plan for self-government that became known as the Fundamental Orders of Connecticut. In 1662, King Charles II recognized Connecticut as a self-governing colony, and the Fundamental Orders became the colony's written constitution.

THE MIDDLE COLONIES

In 1664, King Charles II granted the land between the Connecticut and Delaware rivers to his brother, the Duke of York. The king's main reason for making the grant was to weaken Dutch commercial power in the area. The king sent an expedition that demanded the surrender of the Dutch colony of New Netherland from its governor, Peter Stuyvesant. Stuyvesant's surrender marked the end of Dutch rule in North America.

New York The Duke of York became the **proprietor** of the colony, which was renamed New York. The duke claimed authority over the Dutch and over the Swedes who were living in the area to the south, in present-day Delaware. Control of Delaware later was transferred to the colony of Pennsylvania. In 1703, Delaware became a separate colony.

New Jersey Even before the Duke of York took possession of his colony, he gave part of it to two of his favorite supporters at court—Sir George Carteret and Lord John Berkeley. These two proprietors named their colony New Jersey. In 1702, New Jersey became a royal colony.

Pennsylvania King Charles II of England owed Admiral William Penn a large of money. When the admiral died, the king owed this debt to the admiral's son, also named William. The younger William Penn was a **Quaker,** a member of the Society of Friends, a religious group that opposed wars and fighting. The Quakers also refused to swear allegiance to the English crown. Because Quakers were not welcome in England, they looked to America as a new home.

The king chose to pay his debt to William Penn by granting him, in 1681, a large tract of land in the Americas north of the colony of Maryland. There, Penn could establish a colony for the Quakers. Penn looked upon his colony as a "holy experiment," a place where he could create a refuge for his fellow Quakers and a "city of brotherly love" where people could live in peace and prosperity.

In 1682, Penn and the first Quaker settlers arrived in the new colony. Because Penn did not believe in fighting or in taking land and goods that did not belong to him, he bought the land for his new colony from the local Delaware Indians. The settlers and the Indians lived in peace for about 75 years. Penn named the capital city of the colony Philadelphia; the name means "brotherly love." From a population of about 2,000 in 1682, Pennsylvania grew to about 12,000 people by 1689.

Penn was determined that the persecuted of all religions might find a safe home in Pennsylvania and enrich the colony. He advertised in Europe in the hope of attracting colonists, and word of his policy of religious toleration reached many potential settlers. Before long, a continuous stream of **immigrants** began to flow into

S–V

Pennsylvania from England, Ireland, and the German states. Penn's holy experiment grew and prospered as the years passed, and Pennsylvania became the richest colony in North America.

THE SOUTHERN COLONIES

Virginia, the first southern colony, was founded in 1607 with the establishment of Jamestown. Between 1632 and 1733, four more southern colonies were established: Maryland, North Carolina, South Carolina, and Georgia.

Maryland In 1632, King Charles I carved Maryland from Virginia and granted the land to George Calvert, the First Lord Baltimore. The colony was to be established for Catholics who wanted to settle in the Americas. Before the first colonists could be sent to the new colony, however, George Calvert died. His son, Cecil Calvert, the second Lord Baltimore, continued his father's work.

Because the number of English Catholics was relatively small, Protestants eventually made up the majority of the first settlers. To protect religious freedom, in 1649, the colony passed a Toleration Act. This law allowed all Christian settlers to worship as they wished. Near the end of the seventeenth century, however, the Anglican Church—the Church of England—became the official church of the colony.

The Carolinas In 1663, several influential English nobles at King Charles II's court received **charters** to colonize in Carolina—a vast area that extended southward from Virginia. These colonial proprietors were chiefly con-

cerned with financial gain, and they were poor administrators. In time, two centers of population developed. One, where many Virginia colonists who were looking for new opportunities settled, was near Albemarle Sound. The other population center was at Charles Town (later called Charleston). This settlement attracted English planters from Barbados, an island in the West Indies. These colonists brought their servants and slaves with them. Carolina was the first of the thirteen colonies to have African slaves from its beginning. Also settling in the southern part of the Carolina colony were French Huguenots, Protestants who fled from France to avoid religious persecution.

The two population centers formed the foundations of what later developed into two separate colonies —North Carolina and South Carolina. In 1719, the people living in the southern part of the Carolinas asked King George I (r. 1714–1727) to end the weak rule of the colony's proprietor. The king took over South Carolina as a royal colony. In 1729, North Carolina also became a royal colony.

Georgia In 1733, James Oglethorpe and his associates founded the last of England's colonies in North America. Oglethorpe was a **humanitarian** who wanted to establish a haven for people who were imprisoned for failing to pay their debts. The British government, which granted Oglethorpe a charter, was motivated by other reasons. It planned to have Georgia, which was named for King George II (r. 1727–1760), serve as a **buffer state** between South Carolina and Spanish

History Speaks

The Maryland Toleration Act, 1649

The Maryland Toleration Act did not bring about complete religious freedom in the colony. As Catholics in originally Catholic Maryland became a minority of the population, they were in danger of being ill-treated by the Protestant majority. The Toleration Act, it was believed, was a way to protect not only Catholics, but also all followers of Christianity.

Forasmuch as in a well governed and Christian Common Wealth matters concerning Religion and the honor of God ought in the first place to bee taken, into serious consideracion and endeavoured to bee settled, Be it therefore ordered and enacted by the Right Honourable Cecilius Lord Baron of Baltemore absolute Lord and Proprietary of this Province with the advise and consent of this Generall Assembly:

That whatsoever person or persons within this Province and the Islands thereunto helonging shall from henceforth blaspheme God, that is Curse him, or deny our Saviour Jesus Christ to bee the sonne of God, or shall deny the holy Trinity the father sonne and holy Ghost, or the Godhead of any of the said Three persons of the Trinity or the Unity of the Godhead, or shall use or utter any reproachfull Speeches, words or language concerning the said Holy Trinity, or any of the said three persons thereof, shalbe punished with death and confiscation or forfeiture of all his or her lands and goods to the Lord Proprietary and his heires. . . .

Florida. The presence of this new British colony, it was hoped, would keep the Spanish from moving farther north. The British government also saw the new colony as a way to relieve the financial burden of maintaining the poor in England.

The first settlers arrived in 1733 and founded Savannah. The colony grew slowly. In the end, it did not become a refuge for debtors. At first, the colonists tried to set up many small farms, but this did not prove successful. The climate of Georgia was favorable for the development of large rice plantations, which eventually came to dominate the colony's **agriculture.** In 1752, Georgia became a royal colony.

See also: Jamestown, Virginia; John Winthrop's *City Upon a Hill* in the "Viewpoints" section**;** *Mayflower, The;*

Mayflower Compact; New England; New Netherland; Tobacco.

FURTHER READING
Hedstrom-Page, Deborah. *From Colonies to Country with George Washington.* Nashville, Tenn.: B&H Publishers, 2007.
McCarthy, Pat. *The Thirteen Colonies from Founding to Revolution in American History.* Berkeley Heights, N.J.: Enslow Publishers, 2004.

Tobacco

An agricultural product that played a key role in the success and economic development of England's thirteen American **colonies.** Tobacco is dried and processed from the fresh leaves of tobacco plants. The tobacco plant probably has grown wild in both North and South America since at least 6000 B.C.E. It was first domesticated by **native peoples** around 3000 B.C.E.

Chewing is one of the oldest ways to consume tobacco leaves. Indians in both North and South America chewed and smoked the leaves of the plant. Tobacco has a long history and tradition among the cultures of Native American peoples.

ORIGIN OF THE NAME

The word *tobacco* can be traced back to the Arawak language group, most likely the Taino language of the Caribbean region. According to the priest Bartolomé de Las Casas, the word in Taino referred either to a roll of tobacco leaves or to the *tabago*, a type of Y-shaped pipe used for sniffing tobacco smoke.

Beginning in the early 1400s, however, similar words in Spanish and Italian often were used to define various medicinal plants. These words had their root in the Arabic word *tabbaq*, for the name of various herbs. The word *tabbaq* dates back to the ninth century.

NATIVE AMERICAN USE

Native peoples of the Americas used tobacco long before the arrival of the European settlers who introduced the practice to Europe, where it became very popular. Native Americans did not always use tobacco recreationally. It was first used as an essential part of a religious ceremony. Among some tribes, tobacco was used only by experienced shamans, or medicine men.

Indians in the eastern part of North America often carried large amounts of tobacco in pouches, because it was a readily accepted trading good. These eastern Indians also smoked tobacco in pipes, either in special, sacred ceremonies or to seal agreements. In general, Indians smoked tobacco at all stages of life, even in childhood. Many Indian peoples believed that tobacco was a gift from the creator and that exhaled tobacco smoke carried one's prayers to heaven.

Among the Indians, uncured tobacco often was eaten or drunk as extracted juice. Religious use of tobacco is still common among many native peoples of the Americas. Among the Cree and Ojibwa of the north-central United States and Canada, for example, tobacco is offered to the creator with prayers. It is also used in **sweat lodges,** in pipe ceremonies, and is sometimes given as a gift. For example, a gift of tobacco is traditional when one asks an Ojibwa elder a question of a spiritual nature.

Because of tobacco's sacred value among many Indian groups, the abuse of tobacco, as in chain smoking, is looked down on. Among the Algonquins of Canada, for example, it is believed that if someone abuses tobacco, it will abuse that person in return and cause illness.

ARRIVAL OF THE EUROPEANS

With the arrival of Europeans, tobacco eventually became an essential **cash crop,** especially in the region that became England's southern colonies. The desire to increase tobacco production was one cause of early conflicts between the Indians and European settlers, who often tried to enslave the Indians to work in the tobacco fields. The need for laborers on tobacco plantations later became a major reason to bring African slaves to the colonies.

In 1609, John Rolfe arrived at the fragile Jamestown colony in Virginia. Originally, the tobacco raised in Virginia did not suit European tastes, but Rolfe raised a more popular variety that he grew from seeds that he brought with him from the Caribbean island of Trinidad. John Rolfe is often given credit for saving the Jamestown settlement by finding a crop that could be grown successfully for commercial sale in Europe.

The Virginia settlers also used tobacco as a form of currency for many years. John Rolfe made his fortune by farming tobacco for export at his Varina Farms plantation near Jamestown. In 1616, when Rolfe returned to England with his wife, Pocahontas, a daughter of the Indian chief Powhatan, he was a wealthy man.

Rolfe returned to Jamestown in 1617 after his wife's death in England. Back at his plantation, he continued to work to improve the quality of commercial tobacco. By 1620, about 40,000 pounds (18,000 kilograms) of tobacco were being shipped to England per year. At the time of John Rolfe's death in 1622, Jamestown was thriving as a producer and exporter of tobacco, and the town's population had reached 4,000.

The importation of tobacco into Europe did not occur without debate, even in the early seventeenth century. In 1604, King James I (r. 1603–1625) of England criticized the increasing use of tobacco, noting that it was

> [a] custome lothsome to the eye, hatefull to the Nose, harmefull to the braine, dangerous to the Lungs, and in the blacke stinking fume thereof, neerest resembling the horrible Stigian smoke of the pit that is bottomelesse.

In that same year, a new English law was passed that placed a high tax on every pound of tobacco brought into England.

THE SPREAD OF TOBACCO

During the 1600s and 1700s, tobacco remained the premier cash crop of Virginia, and its cultivation spread to the Carolinas, as well. Large tobacco warehouses filled the areas near the shipping docks of thriving new towns such as Dumfries, on the Potomac River, Richmond, and Manchester.

Tobacco in the Northern Colonies Some northern colonies also grew tobacco. Connecticut and Massachusetts were the two most important of these. Long before Europeans arrived in the New England area, Indians harvested the wild tobacco plants that grew along the banks of the Connecticut River. The tobacco grown in the northern colonies was known as "shade tobacco." Today, it is used as the outer wrappers for cigars.

See also: Jamestown, Virginia; London Company; Slavery and the Slave Trade; Thirteen Colonies.

FURTHER READING
Bruchac, James. *Pocahontas.* New York: Silver Whistle/Harcourt Trade, 2003.
Gatley, Iain. *Tobacco: A Cultural History of How an Exotic Plant Seduced Civilization.* New York: Grove Press, 2003.
Tormey, James. *John Rolfe of Virginia.* Silver Spring, Md.: Beckham Publications, 2006.

Vespucci, Amerigo (1451?–1512)

Explorer for whom the American continents are named. Amerigo Vespucci was born in 1451 or 1454 into a wealthy family in the city of Florence, Italy. As a young man, he read widely and collected maps. He began to work for local bankers and in 1492 was sent to Seville, in Spain, to look after his employer's business interests.

In 1508, King Ferdinand of Spain (r. 1479–1516) made Vespucci the pilot major of Spain. The king commissioned him to start a school for navigators at his home. Earning a huge salary, Vespucci was to standardize and modernize the navigation techniques used by all Spanish sea captains. At the school, Vespucci developed a fairly accurate method for finding longitude.

VOYAGES
Many historians believe that the first voyage of Amerigo Vespucci took place in 1497, probably on a trip organized by King Ferdinand. The king wanted to determine how far the mainland was from the island of Hispaniola, which had been discovered by Christopher Columbus. The captain of this expedition, which set sail in May 1497, was Vicente Yañez Pinzón, who had been captain of the *Niña* on Columbus's first voyage. According to a letter written by Vespucci after this voyage, the expedition reached land at 16 degrees north latitude, probably on the coast of present-day Nicaragua. They then traveled along the Central American coast before returning to the Atlantic Ocean by way of the Straits of Florida, between Florida and Cuba.

Around 1499 or 1500, Vespucci joined another expedition of two ships in the service of Spain. Alonso de Ojeda was in charge of the fleet. After reaching land on the coast of what is now Guyana in South America, for some unknown reason, the two ships separated. Vespucci sailed southward and discovered the mouth of the Amazon River. He then turned around and sighted the island of Trinidad and the Orinoco River, in present-day Venezuela. After stopping at Hispaniola, he returned to Spain in September 1500.

On his third and fourth voyages, Vespucci sailed for the Portuguese government. In May 1501, he sailed from Lisbon, the Portuguese capital, to Cape Verde. From there, he sailed westward until, on January 1, 1502, he reached a gulf on the coast of what is today Brazil. He named it the gulf of Bahia de Todos Santos. Today, it is the site of the city of Bahia, Brazil. From Bahia, he coasted along South

America, most likely as far south as the present-day Rio de la Plata in Argentina. On his return, he discovered the South Atlantic island known today as South Georgia. He returned to Lisbon in September 1502.

In late 1502 or 1503, Vespucci set forth on his last voyage, again in the service of Portugal. Departing from Lisbon, the fleet sailed west to Cape Verde. The ships continued westward and again reached the coast of Brazil. From there, they sailed south along the coast of South America to the site of present-day Rio de Janeiro. Vespucci claimed that the expedition sailed much farther south and reached what is today Patagonia in Argentina. Some historians doubt that the fleet sailed this far south, however, because Portuguese maps of South America created after this voyage do not show any land south of present-day São Paulo, in southern Brazil.

NAMING THE CONTINENTS

As Vespucci sailed back to Lisbon after his last voyage, he wrote to his friends and former employers in Italy, the powerful Medici family. In the letter, he noted that the landmasses that he and his crew explored were much larger than they expected and that the lands were very different from the Asia described by earlier Europeans. Vespucci concluded that it must be a "New World"—a previously unknown fourth continent, after Europe, Asia, and Africa.

The publication and circulation of this letter led the German mapmaker Martin Waldseemüller to name the new continent "America" on the world map he created in 1507. Vespucci had used a Latinized form of his name, Americus Vespucius, in his Latin writings. Waldseemüller used that name, *Americus,* as the base for the name of the new continent, giving the name the feminine form *America.*

Waldseemüller printed a woodblock map with the name "America" across the southern continent of this New World. He printed and sold a thousand copies of his map throughout Europe A 1538 world map by the Flemish mapmaker Gerardus Mercator was the first to label North America and South America.

Amerigo Vespucci died of malaria in Seville, Spain, on February 22, 1512. He was between 58 and 61 years old.

See also: Columbus, Christopher; Ferdinand and Isabella; Magellan, Ferdinand; Portugal; Spain.

FURTHER READING

Fernandez-Armesto, Felipe. *Amerigo: The Man Who Gave His Name to America.* New York: Random House, 2008.

Lambert, Lorene. *Who in the World Was the Forgotten Explorer?: The Story of Amerigo Vespucci.* Charles City, Va.: Peace Hill Press, 2005.

S–V

✉ *From* **The Diversity of Native America,** *Juan de Oñate, 1599*

In 1598, the Spanish explorer Juan de Oñate moved north from Mexico to what is today the American Southwest. He brought with him more than 100 soldiers, several slaves, eight Franciscan missionaries, and about 7,000 cattle. In this 1599 letter, he describes the **native peoples** he encountered.

" The people are as a rule of good disposition, generally of the color of those of New Spain, and almost the same in customs, dress, grinding of meal, food, dances, songs, and in many other respects. This is not true of their languages, which here are numerous and different from those in Mexico. Their religion consists in worshipping of idols, of which they have many; in their temples they worship them in their own way with fire, painted reeds, feathers, and general offerings of almost everything: little animals, birds, vegetables, etc. Their government is one of complete freedom, for although they have some chieftains they obey them badly and in very few matters.

We have seen other nations, such as Querechos or Vaqueros, who live among the Cibola [Pueblo Indians] in tents of tanned hides. The Apaches, some of whom we also saw, are extremely numerous. Although I was told that they lived in rancherias, in recent days I have learned that they live in pueblos the same as the people here. . . . They are a people that has not yet publicly rendered obedience to his majesty. . . . Because of failure to exercise as much caution as was necessary, my maese de campo and twelve companions were killed at a fortress pueblo named Acoma, which must have contained three thousand Indians more or less. In punishment of their wickedness and treason to his majesty. . . and as a warning to others, I razed and burned their pueblo. . . . "

✉ *From* **The Opening of the Fur Trade,** *Samuel de Champlain, 1604*

Although the French claimed the St. Lawrence River Valley in the 1530s, the profitable fur trade did not become established until the early 1600s. In this 1604 letter, the French explorer explains how he convinced the Indians to join with the French in the fur trade.

> ❝ . . .I went on shore with my companions and two of our savages who served as interpreters. I directed the men in our barque [boat] to approach near the savages, and hold their arms in readiness to do their duty in case they notice any movement of these people against us. Bessabez [the chief], seeing us on land, bade us sit down, and began to smoke with his companions. . . . They presented us with venison and game.
>
> I directed our interpreter to say to our savages that. . .Sieur de Monts [Champlain's patron] had sent me to see them, and. . .that he desired to inhabit their country and show them how to cultivate it, in order that they might not continue to lead so miserable a life as they were doing. . . .They expressed their great satisfaction, saying that no greater good could come to them than to have our friendship, and that they desired to live in peace with their enemies, and that we should dwell in their land, in order that they might in the future more than ever before engage in hunting beavers, and give us a part of them in return for our providing them with things which they wanted. . . . ❞

✱ London Company (or Virginia Company) Charter, 1606

With the London Company Charter, King James I (r. 1603–1625) granted several of his loyal subjects permission to start a **colony** in the land known as Virginia. The **charter** defines the boundaries of the Virginia colony in the second paragraph.

The third paragraph notes that the **colonists** will bring the Christian religion to the **native peoples.** The fourth paragraph extends the western boundary of the colony to the north and northeast; it also notes that no other English colonists will be granted permission to settle in the same area, except with the approval of the colony's council. Without the London Company Charter, the men of the company had no legal authorization to settle or trade in Virginia.

> *I JAMES,* by the Grace of God, King of *England, Scotland, France* and *Ireland,* Defender of the Faith, &c. WHEREAS our loving and well-disposed Subjects, Sir *Thomas Gates,* and Sir *George Somers,* Knights, *Richard Hackluit,* Prebendary of *Westminster,* and *Edward-Maria Wingfield, Thomas Hanham,* and *Ralegh Gilbert,* Esqrs. *William Parker,* and *George Popham,* Gentlemen, and divers others of our loving Subjects, have been humble Suitors unto us, that We would vouchsafe unto them our Licence, to make Habitation, Plantation, and to deduce a Colony of sundry of our People into that Part of *America,* commonly called VIRGINIA, and other Parts and Territories in *America,* either appertaining unto us, or which are not now actually possessed by any *Christian* Prince or People, situate, lying, and being all along the Sea Coasts, between four and thirty Degrees of *Northerly* Latitude from the Equinoctial Line, and five and forty Degrees of the same Latitude, and in the main Land between the same four and thirty and five and forty Degrees, and the Islands thereunto adjacent, or within one hundred Miles of the Coasts thereof;
>
> II. And to that End, and for the more speedy Accomplishment of their said intended Plantation and Habitation there, are desirous to divide themselves into two several Colonies and Companies; The one consisting of certain Knights, Gentlemen, Merchants, and other Adventurers, of our City of *London* and elsewhere, which are, and from time to time shall be, joined unto them, which do desire to begin their Plantation and Habitation in some fit and convenient Place, between four and thirty and one and forty Degrees of the said Latitude, along the Coasts of *Virginia* and Coasts of *America* aforesaid; And the other consisting of sundry Knights, Gentlemen, Merchants, and other Adventurers, of our Cities of *Bristol* and *Exeter,* and of our Town of

Plimouth, and of other Places, which do join themselves unto that Colony, which do desire to begin their Plantation and Habitation in some fit and convenient Place, between eight and thirty Degrees and five and forty Degrees of the said Latitude, all alongst the said Coast of *Virginia* and *America,* as that Coast lyeth:

III. We, greatly commending, and graciously accepting of, their Desires for the Furtherance of so noble a Work, which may, by the Providence of Almighty God, hereafter tend to the Glory of his Divine Majesty, in propagating of *Christian* Religion to such People, as yet live in Darkness and miserable Ignorance of the true Knowledge and Worship of God, and may in time bring the Infidels and Savages, living in those Parts, to human Civility, and to a settled and quiet Government; DO, by these our Letters Patents, graciously accept of, and agree to, their humble and well-intended Desires;

IV. And do therefore, for Us, our Heirs, and Successors GRANT and agree, that the said Sir *Thomas Gates,* Sir *George Somers, Richard Hackluit,* and *Edward-Maria Wingfield,* Adventurers of and for our City of *London,* and all such others, as are, or shall be, joined unto them of that Colony, shall be called the *first* Colony; And they shall and may begin their said first Plantation and Habitation, at any Place upon the said Coast of *Virginia* or *America,* where they shall think fit and convenient, between the said four and thirty and one and forty Degrees of the said Latitude; And that they shall have all the Lands, Woods, Soil, Grounds, Havens, Ports, Rivers, Mines,

Minerals, Marshes, Waters, Fishings, Commodities, and Hereditaments, whatsoever, from the said first Seat of their Plantation and Habitation by the space of fifty Miles of *English* Statute Measure, all along the said Coast of *Virginia* and *America,* towards the *West* and *Southwest,* as the Coast lyeth, with all the Islands within one hundred Miles directly over against the same Sea Coast; And also all the Lands, Soil, Grounds, Havens, Ports, Rivers, Mines, Minerals, Woods, Waters, Marshes, Fishings, Commodities, and Hereditaments, whatsoever, from the said Place of their first Plantation and Habitation for the space of fifty like English *Miles* all alongst the said Coast of *Virginia* and *America,* towards the *East and Northeast,* or towards the *North,* as the Coast lyeth, together with all the Islands within one hundred Miles, directly over against the said Sea Coast; And also all the Lands, Woods, Soil, Grounds, Havens, Ports, Rivers, Mines, Minerals, Marshes, Waters, Fishings, Commodities, and Hereditaments, whatsoever, from the same fifty Miles every way on the Sea Coast, directly into the main Land by the Space of one hundred like *English* Miles; And shall and may inhabit and remain there; and shall and may also build and fortify within any the same, for their better Safeguard and Defence, according to their best Discretion, and the Discretion of the Council of that Colony; And that no other of our Subjects shall be permitted, or suffered, to plant or inhabit behind, or on the Backside of them, towards the main Land, without the Express License or Consent of the Council of that Colony, thereunto in Writing first had and obtained. **99**

📖 From City Upon a Hill (A Model of Christian Charity), *John Winthrop, 1630*

In 1630, Reverend John Winthrop wrote and then delivered his sermon "A Model of Christian Charity" while still onboard the *Arabella,* heading toward the Massachusetts colony. In the sermon, he describes his vision of a peaceful Christian community that would be served by good government.

> Thus stands the cause between God and us. We are entered into covenant with Him for this work. We have taken out a commission. The Lord hath given us leave to draw our own articles. We have professed to enterprise these and those accounts, upon these and those ends. We have hereupon besought Him of favor and blessing. Now if the Lord shall please to hear us, and bring us in peace to the place we desire, then hath He ratified this covenant and sealed our commission, and will expect a strict performance of the articles contained in it; but if we shall neglect the observation of these articles which are the ends we have propounded, and, dissembling with our God, shall fall to embrace this present world and prosecute our carnal intentions, seeking great things for ourselves and our posterity, the Lord will surely break out in wrath against us, and be revenged of such a people, and make us know the price of the breach of such a covenant.
>
> Now the only way to avoid this shipwreck, and to provide for our posterity, is to follow the counsel of Micah, to do justly, to love mercy, to walk humbly with our God. For this end, we must be knit together, in this work, as one man. We must entertain each other in brotherly affection. We must be willing to abridge ourselves of our superfluities, for the supply of others' necessities. We must uphold a familiar commerce together in all meekness, gentleness, patience and liberality. We must delight in each other; make others' conditions our own; rejoice together, mourn together, labor and suffer together, always having before our eyes our commission and community in the work, as members of the same body. So shall we keep the unity of the spirit in the bond of peace. The Lord will be our God, and delight to dwell among us, as His own people, and will command a blessing upon us in all our ways, so that we shall see much more of His wisdom, power, goodness and truth, than formerly we have been acquainted with. We shall find that the God of Israel is among us, when ten of us shall be able to resist a thousand of our enemies; when He shall make us a praise and glory that men shall say of succeeding plantations, "may the Lord make it like that of New England." For we must consider that we shall be as a city upon a hill. The eyes of all people are upon us. So that if we shall deal falsely with our God in this work we have undertaken, and so cause Him to withdraw His present help from us, we shall be made a story and a by-word through the world. We shall open the mouths of enemies to speak evil of the ways of God, and all professors for God's sake. We shall shame the faces of many of God's worthy servants, and cause their prayers to be turned into curses upon us till we be consumed out of the good land whither we are going.

🌟 *William Penn's Charter, 1681*

King Charles II (r. 1660–1685) granted William Penn, a wealthy Englishman, and his heirs a huge tract of land "not yet cultivated and planted," which later became the colonies of Pennsylvania and Delaware. Section I defines the boundaries of this land grant; Section II gives Penn and his descendents the rights to all the natural resources of the **colony.**

> Charles the Second, by the grace of God King of England, Scotland, France and Ireland, defender of the faith, &c., To all to whome these presents shall come Greeting. Whereas our Trustie and well beloved Subject, William Penn, Esquire, sonn and heire of Sir William Penn, deceased, out of a commendable desire to enlarge our English Empire, and promote such usefull commodities as may bee of benefit to us and our Dominions, as alsoe to reduce the Savage Natives by gentle and just manners to the love of civill Societie and Christian Religion hath humbley besought leave of vs to transport an ample colonie vnto a certaine Countrey hereinafter described in the partes of America not yet cultivated and planted. And hath likewise humbley besought our Royall majestie to give grant, and confirme all the said countrey with certaine priviledges and Jurisdiccions requisite for the good Government and saffie of the said Countrey and Colonie, to him and his heires forever.
>
> [Section I] Know Yee, therefore, that wee, favouring the petition and good purpose of the said William Penn, and having regard to the memorie and merits of his late father, in divers services, and perticulerly to his conduct, courage and discretion vnder our dearest brother, James Duke of Yorke, in that signall battell and victorie, fought and obteyned against the Dutch fleeter commanded by the Heer Van Opdam, in the yeare One thousand six hundred sixtie five, in consideration thereof our special grace, certaine knowledge and mere motion, Have given and granted, and by this our present Charter, for vs, our heires and sucessors, Doe give and grant unto the said William Penn, his heires and assignes all that tract or parte of land in America, with all the Islands therein conteyned, as the same is bounded on the East by Delaware River, from twelve miles distance, Northwarde of New Castle Towne unto the three and fortieth degree of Northern latitude if the said River doeth extend soe farre Northwards; but if the said River shall not extend soe farre Northward, then by the said River soe farr as it doth extend, and from the head of the said River the Easterne bounds are to bee determined by a meridian line, to bee drawn from the head of the said River vnto the said three and fortieth degree, the said lands to extend Westwards, five degrees in longitude, to bee computed from the said Easterne Bounds, and the said lands to bee bounded on the North, by the beginning of the three and fortieth degree of Northern latitude, and on

(continues)

(continued)

the south, by a circle drawne at twelve miles, distance from New Castle Northwards, and Westwards vnto the beginning of the fortieth degree of Northerne Latitude; and then by a straight line Westwards, to the limit of Longitude above menconed.

[Section II] Wee Doe alsoe give and grant vnto the said William Penn, his heires and assignes, the free and vndisturbed vse, and continuance in and passage into and out of all and singular Ports, harbours, Bayes, waters, rivers, Isles and Inletts, belonging vnto or leading to and from the Countrey, or Islands aforesaid; and all the soyle, lands, fields, woods, vnder-woods, mountains, hills, fenns, Isles, Lakes, Rivers, waters, rivulets, Bays and Inletts, scituate or being within or belonging vnto the Limitts and Bounds aforesaid together with the fishing of all sortes of fish, whales, sturgeons, and all Royall and other fishes in the sea, bayes, Inletts, waters or Rivers, within the premises, and the fish therein taken, and alsoe all veines, mines and quarries, as well discovered as not discovered, of Gold, Silver, Gemms and pretious Stones, and all other whatsoever, stones, metals, or of any other thing or matter whatsoever, found or to bee found within the Countrey, Isles, or Limitts aforesaid. . . **,,**

✸ Treaty of Paris of 1763

The Treaty of Paris of 1763, which ended the French and Indian War, gave all French lands west of the Mississippi River as well as all of Canada to Great Britain. France was allowed to keep a few small islands off the Canadian coast and retain the right to fish in the Gulf of St. Lawrence. The treaty firmly established British control of much of North America. It also set the stage for the disagreements between the **colonists** and the British government that led to the American Revolution.

" **IV.** His Most Christian Majesty renounces all pretensions which he has heretofore formed or might have formed to Nova Scotia or Acadia in all its parts, and guaranties the whole of it, and with all its dependencies, to the King of Great Britain: Moreover, his Most Christian Majesty cedes and guaranties to his said Britannick Majesty, in full right, Canada, with all its dependencies, as well as the island of Cape Breton, and all the other islands and coasts in the gulph and river of St. Lawrence, and in general, every thing that depends on the said countries, lands, islands, and coasts, with the sovereignty, property, possession, and all rights acquired by treaty, or otherwise, which the Most Christian King and the Crown of France have had till now over the said countries, lands, islands, places, coasts, and their inhabitants, so that the Most Christian King cedes and makes over the whole to the said King, and to the Crown of Great Britain, and that in the most ample manner and form, without restriction, and without any liberty to depart from the said cession and guaranty under any pretence, or to disturb Great Britain in the possessions above mentioned. His Britannick Majesty, on his side, agrees to grant the liberty of the Catholick religion to the inhabitants of Canada: he will, in consequence, give the most precise and most effectual orders, that his new Roman Catholic subjects may profess the worship of their religion according to the rites of the Romish church, as far as the laws of Great Britain permit. His Britannick Majesty farther agrees, that the French inhabitants, or others who had been subjects of the Most Christian King in Canada, may retire with all safety and freedom wherever they shall think proper, and may sell their estates, provided it be to the subjects of his Britannick Majesty, and bring away their effects as well as their persons, without being restrained in their emigration, under any pretence whatsoever, except that of debts or of criminal prosecutions: The term lim-

ited for this emigration shall be fixed to the space of eighteen months, to be computed from the day of the exchange of the ratification of the present treaty.

V. The subjects of France shall have the liberty of fishing and drying on a part of the coasts of the island of Newfoundland, such as it is specified in the XIIIth article of the treaty of Utrecht; which article is renewed and confirmed by the present treaty, (except what relates to the island of Cape Breton, as well as to the other islands and coasts in the mouth and in the gulph of St. Lawrence:) And his Britannick Majesty consents to leave to the subjects of the Most Christian King the liberty of fishing in the gulph of St. Lawrence, on condition that the subjects of France do not exercise the said fishery but at the distance of three leagues from all the coasts belonging to Great Britain, as well those of the continent as those of the islands situated in the said gulph of St. Lawrence. And as to what relates to the fishery on the coasts of the island of Cape Breton, out of the said gulph, the subjects of the Most Christian King shall not be permitted to exercise the said fishery but at the distance of fifteen leagues from the coasts of the island of Cape Breton; and the fishery on the coasts of Nova Scotia or Acadia, and every where else out of the said gulph, shall remain on the foot of former treaties.

"

✸ *Proclamation of 1763*

Great Britain's King George III (r. 1760–1820) issued the Proclamation of 1763. He wanted to prevent English settlers from moving westward into
the Ohio River Valley as a way to keep peace with
the Indians in the region. The settlers in the thirteen
British Colonies greatly resented the restrictions
that the proclamation placed on them.

" And whereas it is just and rea-
sonable, and essential to our
interest and the security of our
colonies, that the several nations or tribes of Indians with
whom we are connected, and who
live under our protection, should not
be molested or disturbed in the possession of such parts of our domin-
ions and territories as, not having
been ceded to or purchased by us,
are reserved to them, or any of them,
as their hunting-grounds; we do
therefore, with the advice of our
Privy Council, declare it to be our
royal will and pleasure, that. . . as
aforesaid, are reserved to the said
Indians, or any of them.

And we do further declare it to be
our royal will and pleasure, for the
present as aforesaid, to reserve under
our sovereignty, protection, and dominion, for the use of the said Indians, all the land and territories. . .
lying to the westward of the sources
of the rivers which fall into the sea
from the west and northwest as
aforesaid; and we do hereby strictly
forbid, on pain of our displeasure, all
our loving subjects from making any
purchases or settlements whatever, or
taking possession of any of the lands
above reserved, without our special
leave and license for that purpose
first obtained.

RESTRICTIONS ON SETTLEMENT
And we do further strictly enjoin and
require all persons whatever, who
have either willfully or inadvertently
seated themselves upon any lands
within the countries above described,
or upon any other lands which, not
having been ceded to or purchased
by us, are still reserved to the said
Indians as aforesaid, forthwith to
remove themselves from such
settlements.

RESOLUTION OF INDIAN PROBLEMS
And whereas great frauds and abuses
have been committed in the purchas-
ing lands of the Indians, to the great
prejudice of our interests, and to the
great dissatisfaction of the said Indians; in order, therefore, to prevent
such irregularities for the future, and
to the end that the Indians may be
convinced of our justice and determined resolution to remove all rea-
sonable cause of discontent, we do,
with the advice of our Privy Council,
strictly enjoin and require, that no
private person do presume to make
any purchase from the said Indians of
any lands reserved to the said Indians
within those parts of our colonies
where we have thought proper to
allow settlement; but that if at any
time any of the said Indians should
be inclined to dispose of the said

lands, the same shall be purchased only for us, in our name, at some public meeting or assembly of the said Indians, to be held for that purpose by the Governor or commander in chief of our colony respectively within which they shall lie: and in case they shall lie within the limits of any proprietary government, they shall be purchased only for the use and in the name of such proprietaries, conformable to such directions and instructions as we or they shall think proper to give for that purpose. And we do, by the advice of our Privy Council, declare and enjoin, that the trade with the said Indians shall be free and open to all our subjects whatever, provided that every person who may incline to trade with the said Indians do take out a license for carrying on such trade, from the Governor or commander in chief of any of our colonies respectively where such person shall reside, and also give security to observe such regulations as we shall at any time think fit, by ourselves or commissaries to be appointed for this purpose, to direct and appoint for the benefit of the said trade. And we do hereby authorize, enjoin, and require the Governors and commanders in chief of all our colonies respectively, as well those under our immediate government as those under the government and direction of proprietaries, to grant such licenses without fee or reward, taking especial care to insert therein a condition that such license shall be void, and the security forfeited, in case the person to whom the same is granted shall refuse or neglect to observe such regulations as we shall think proper to prescribe as aforesaid.

And we do further expressly enjoin and require all officers whatever, as well military as those employed in the management and direction of Indian affairs within the territories reserved as aforesaid, for the use of the said Indians, to seize and apprehend all persons whatever who, standing charged with treasons, misprisions of treason, murders, or other felonies or misdemeanors, shall fly from justice and take refuge in the said territory, and to send them under a proper guard to the colony where the crime was committed of which they shall stand accused, in order to take their trial for the same.

Given at our Court at St. James's, the 7th day of October 1763, in the third year of our reign.

"

✉ Letter to Reverend Samson Occum, Phillis Wheatley, 1774

In 1765, when Phillis Wheatley, an African American poet, was about 11 years old, she wrote a letter to Reverend Samson Occum. Occum was a Mohegan Indian and an ordained Presbyterian minister. Wheatley's letter led to a friendship with Occum, who was also a poet, and who later published an Indian hymnal. On February 11, 1774, Wheatley again wrote Occum, commenting on a criticism he had written of slave-holding Christian ministers.

> Rev'd and honor'd Sir,
>
> I have this day received your obliging kind Epistle, and am greatly satisfied with your Reasons respecting the Negroes, and think highly reasonable what you offer in Vindication of their natural Rights: Those that invade them cannot be insensible that the divine Light is chasing away the thick Darkness which broods over the Land of Africa; and the Chaos which has reign'd so long, is converting into beautiful Order, and [r]eveals more and more clearly, the glorious Dispensation of civil and religious Liberty, which are so inseparably Limited, that there is little or no Enjoyment of one Without the other: Otherwise, perhaps, the Israelites had been less solicitous for their Freedom from Egyptian slavery; I do not say they would have been contented without it, by no means, for in every human Breast, God has implanted a Principle, which we call Love of Freedom; it is impatient of Oppression, and pants for Deliverance; and by the Leave of our modern Egyptians I will assert, that the same Principle lives in us. God grant Deliverance in his own Way and Time, and get him honour upon all those whose Avarice impels them to countenance and help forward tile Calamities of their fellow Creatures. This I desire not for their Hurt, but to convince them of the strange Absurdity of their Conduct whose Words and Actions are so diametrically, opposite. How well the Cry for Liberty, and the reverse Disposition for the exercise of oppressive Power over others agree, — I humbly think it does not require the Penetration of a Philosopher to determine.—

abolish To do away with; annul; to destroy completely.

abolititonists People who wished to do away with slavery.

agriculture The production of crops from the land; farming.

alliances Associations formed for the benefit of those involved.

allies People or countries with whom one has made a pact of mutual support.

annexed Taken over and subordinated.

archeologists Scholars and scientists who specialize in the study of ancient cultures and life-forms.

autonomy The ability to be self-ruling or to function without outside influence.

balance of trade The difference, in monetary value, between a nation's exports and its imports.

bankrupt Unable to pay off debt; also, having a complete lack of the resources needed to keep a business running.

booty Treasure taken as spoils of war or piracy.

British crown The king or queen of Great Britain.

broadsheets Single-sheet publications that reported on current events, sometimes by means of ballads, political satires, or other entertaining forms.

buffer state Typically, a neutral state that acts as a barrier between two conflicting states.

cash crop A crop grown for the purpose of making a monetary profit.

cede Give control or ownership of a piece of land to another nation.

charter A written contract that creates cities and governing bodies and that guarantees rights and privileges.

circumnavigate Sail around the globe.

colonial era A period of time, from the sixteenth century to the eighteenth century, during which European nations established and maintained colonies in other parts of the world in search of power and wealth.

colonists People who move from their homelands to settle in a new territories—colonies—controlled by the parent country.

colony A territory, town, or city established in a new land but controlled by a parent country.

confederation A group of states or colonies that come together to work towards a common goal.

conquistador One of the explorers who conquered Mexico and Peru for Spain in the sixteenth century.

Counter-Reformation A period of time, in the sixteenth and seventeenth centuries, during which the Catholic Church made efforts to combat the Protestant Reformation.

dependencies Lands that are reliant upon a stronger country or nation for support or protection.

drawing and quartering Method of punishment in which the victim is dragged to the gallows by a horse and, at some point, has his body split into four parts.

economies of scale The lowering of the price of a product because of an increase in the output of the product.

equator The line of latitude halfway between the North and South poles; the equator divides the earth into the Northern and Southern hemispheres.

exported Shipped to other countries to be sold.

famine An extreme lack of food in an area that often results in mass starvation.

fathom A unit of measurement used to measure the depth of water; six feet equal one fathom.

fireship A ship loaded with explosives and sent adrift among enemy ships to damage or destroy them.

frontier The land that acts as a border between settled and unsettled land.

galleon A large Spanish warship or merchant vessel of the colonial era.

Glorious Revolution A bloodless revolution that removed King James II (r. 1685–1688) from the throne of England and replaced him with his daughter, Mary II (r. 1689–1694), and her husband, William III (r. 1689–1702).

Habsburg Dynasty A royal German family that ruled Spain from the early 1500s to 1700; during that time, the Habsburgs also ruled over Austria, Hungary, and Bohemia.

hemispheres Halves of the globe.

hereditary Passed down from generation to generation in a family line.

House of Burgesses A representative assembly in colonial Virginia that was the first such assembly in the Americas.

humanitarian A person who is interested in helping to promote the welfare of his or her fellow citizens.

Iberian Peninsula The mass of land in Western Europe that contains Spain and Portugal; bordered on the north and west by the Atlantic Ocean and on the south and east by the Mediterranean Sea.

immigrants People who move away from their countries of origin to settle in other countries.

immortal Living forever.

import A product or other object of commerce that is brought into a country to be sold there; also, the act of bringing in, or importing, such goods.

indentured servants People who are bound by contracts, called indentures, to work for other people for stated periods of time, usually in exchange for something else, such as passage to a colony.

industrial revolution The change to mechanized production of goods that took place in England in the late eighteenth century.

inflation A rise in prices related to a rise in the amount of money available to spend in a country or other location.

irrigation The use of artificial channels and streams to carry water to and through a piece a of land to make it available for planting.

isthmus A small strip of land that connects two larger bodies of land and that is surrounded on both sides by bodies of water.

joint-stock company A company that sells shares of ownership in itself to numerous investors.

laissez-faire Describes an economic system in which the government has little involvement, allowing people to operate their businesses and trade as they please.

league A unit of measurement; three miles equal one league.

longhouses Long, communal dwellings built by some Native American peoples.

malaria A parasitic disease, spread by mosquitoes, that results in chills and fever.

mercenary A person who is hired to fight in the military forces of a foreign country.

middle class Group of people between the upper and lower classes of a society, typically consisting of businesspeople and skilled workers.

migrants People who move regularly to find work.

migrate Move from one habitat or country to another.

militia A group of citizens organized for military service.

missionaries People who travel throughout an area or to foreign countries to convert others to their religious beliefs.

monarch A person, such as a king or queen, who rules over a kingdom.

monopoly Exclusive ownership or control of a particular good or market.

monsoon A periodic wind in the Indian Ocean; also the torrential rainfall that usually accompanies this wind.

mutiny Forcible revolt against a superior officer or governor.

native peoples Persons born in a particular region, as opposed to immigrants.

Norman Conquest The invasion of England in 1066 by William the Conqueror of Normandy (r. 1066–1087); William formed one of the most powerful monarchies in Europe and was pivotal in the development of modern England.

Northwest Passage Mythical route from the Atlantic Ocean to the Pacific, across the northern part of North America; the passage was sought by explorers from many European nations.

panhandle A narrow projection of land that is part of a larger territory; Florida and Alaska have panhandles.

parallel One of the imaginary lines on the globe, including the equator, that mark degrees of latitude.

patroon system System in the Dutch colony of New Netherland in which 16-mile tracts of land along a river were granted to colonizers.

pillage Loot or plunder, as in war or piracy.

polytheistic A belief in many gods.

privateers Nonmilitary sailors on armed private ships who are hired by governments to attack the shipping of their enemies.

proprietor Someone who is granted ownership of a colony, with the right to establish a government.

Protestant Reformation A movement, started by Martin Luther in 1517, to reform certain practices within the Catholic Church; eventually led to the establishment of independent Protestant sects and churches, including Lutherans, Anglicans, Calvinists, and Presbyterians.

Quakers Popular name for the Religious Society of Friends, a Christian religious group that does not have a creed or clergy but believes in developing religious beliefs on inspiration from God; Quakers are opposed to wars and fighting.

Renaissance European cultural movement that began in the fourteenth century and was characterized by a revival of an interest in the arts of ancient times.

revenue Money generated from the sale of services and goods or from the collection of taxes.

sachem The chief of a North American Indian tribe.

scurvy A condition caused by a lack of vitamin C in the diet. Signs of scurvy include tiredness, joint and muscle aches, and bleeding gums; it was common among sailors deprived of fresh fruits and vegetables while at sea.

secede Withdraw from an organization, usually a political entity.

settler colonies Territories, towns, or cities in a new land that are controlled by a parent country and to which people from the parent country move permanently.

shareholders People who own a portion, or share, of a company.

smelting A process in which ore is heated to separate the ore's metal components.

sole proprietorship A business entity that has no legal distinction from its owner.

specialization in production The idea that by producing one particular item well, a company may keep its costs down and so be able to sell its special product at a more competitive price.

speculating The act of buying and selling goods in an attempt to make money at a later date; speculators are people who assume business risks in the hope of gaining profits.

stockholders People who own a portion of a company.

strait A narrow passage of water that connects two larger bodies of water.

subsistence The bare minimum of an item, such as food or money, needed to survive.

subsistence farming Growing the minimum amount of food necessary to feed oneself and one's family.

surplus The amount left over when one's needs are satisfied.

sweat lodges Huts heated by steam from water poured on hot rocks; sweat lodges are used in rituals by many native peoples of North America.

tariffs Taxes imposed on imported goods.

terraced fields Flat, horizontal areas cut into the side of a hill to increase the amount of cultivatable land.

treason An act of betrayal taken deliberately against a government or official to which one owes allegiance.

tribute Payment, in the form of money or goods, made by the ruler of one nation to the ruler of another nation to show loyalty and submission.

vice-royalty Beginning in the 1500s and continuing through the early 1800s, the area governed by a viceroy in Spain's American colonies.

viceroy The governor of a region or country who rules as the representative of the king or queen of a parent country.

Selected Bibliography

Alonso, Roberto Velesco, *et al. The Aztec Empire*. New York: Guggenheim Museum, 2004.

Ames, Glenn J. *Vasco da Gama: Renaissance Crusader*. London: Longman, 2001.

Anderson, Fred. *The War That Made America: A Short History of the French and Indian War*. New York: Penguin, 2006.

Aronson, Marc. *Sir Walter Raleigh and the Quest for El Dorado*. Boston: Clarion Books, 2000.

Bailey, Katharine. *Vasco da Gama: Quest for the Spice Trade*. New York: Crabtree Books, 2007.

Bawlf, Samuel. *The Secret Voyage of Sir Francis Drake, 1577–1580*. New York: Penguin, 2004.

Bergreen, Laurence. *Over the Edge of the World: Magellan's Terrifying Circumnavigation of the Globe*. New York: Harper Perennial, 2004.

Black, Lydia T. *Russians in Alaska: 1732–1867*. Fairbanks: University of Alaska Press, 2004.

Borneman, Walter R. *The French and Indian War: Deciding the Fate of America*. New York: Harper Perennial, 2007.

Bruchac, James. *Pocahontas*. New York: Silver Whistle/Harcourt Trade, 2003.

Carroll, Joy. *Wolfe and Montcalm: Their Lives, Their Times, and the Fate of a Continent*. Richmond Hill, Ont.: Firefly, 2004.

Champlain, Samuel de. *The Voyages of Samuel de Champlain, Volume 1*. London: Echo Library, 2007.

Chartrand, Rene. *The Forts of New France in Northeast America, 1600–1763*. Oxford: Osprey, 2008.

Chrisp, Peter. *Christopher Columbus*. London: DK Press, 2006.

Deetz, James, and Patricia Scott Deetz. *The Times of Their Lives: Life, Love, and Death in Plymouth Colony*. New York: Anchor, 2001.

DiConsiglio, John. *Francisco Pizarro: Destroyer of the Inca Empire*. New York: Franklin Watts, 2008.

Doak, Robin S. *Christopher Columbus: Explorer of the New World*. Mankato, Minn.: Compass Point Press, 2005.

Edwards, J. *Ferdinand and Isabella: Profiles in Power*. Upper Saddle River, N.J.: Longman, 2004.

Ekelund, Robert B., and Robert D. Tollison. *Politicized Economies: Monarchy, Monopoly, and Mercantilism*. College Station: Texas A&M University, 1997.

Elliot, J.H. *Imperial Spain*. New York: Penguin, 2002.

Frost, Orcutt. *Bering: The Russian Discovery of America*. New Haven, Conn.: Yale University Press, 2003.

Gallagher, Jim. *Hernando de Soto and the Exploration of Florida*. New York: Chelsea House, 2000.

Gatley, Iain. *Tobacco: A Cultural History of How an Exotic Plant Seduced Civilization*. New York: Grove Press, 2003.

Gibson, Karen Bush. *New Netherland: The Dutch Settle the Hudson Valley*. Hockessin, Del.: Mitchell Lane Publishers, 2006.

Gleason, Carrie. *Henry Hudson: Seeking the Northwest Passage*. New York: Crabtree, 2005.

Grizzard, Frank, and D. Boyd Smith. *Jamestown Colony: A Political, Social, and Cultural History*. Santa Barbara, Cal.: ABC-CLIO, 2007.

Hedstrom-Page, Deborah. *From Colonies to Country with George Washington*. Nashville, Tenn.: B&H Publishers, 2007.

Heinrichs, Ann. *De Soto: Hernando de Soto Explores the Southeast.* Mankato, Minn.: Compass Point Press, 2002.

Hibbert, Christopher. *Wolfe at Quebec: The Man Who Won the French and Indian War.* Lanham, Md.: Cooper Square Press, 1999.

Hirschfelder, Arlene B. *Squanto, 1585?–1622.* Mankato, Minn.: Blue Earth Books, 2003.

Hoobler, Dorothy, and Thomas Hoobler. *Captain John Smith: Jamestown and the Birth of the American Dream.* Hoboken, N.J.: John Wiley & Sons, 2006.

Internet School Library Media Center. "Colonial America 1600-1775: K12 Resources." Available online. URL: http://falcon.jmu.edu/~ramseyil/colonial.htm.

Johnson, Caleb. *The Mayflower and Her Passengers.* Philadelphia, Pa.: Xlibris. 2006.

Kamen, Henry. *Empire: How Spain Became a World Power, 1492–1763.* New York: HarperCollins, 2003.

Kamma, Anna. *If You Lived When There Was Slavery in America.* New York: Scholastic, 2004.

Kelso, William M. *Jamestown: The Buried Truth.* Charlottesville: University of Virginia Press, 2006.

Koestler-Grack, Rachel A. *Vasco da Gama and the Sea Route to India.* New York: Chelsea House, 2005.

Kupperman, Karen Ordahl. *The Jamestown Project.* Cambridge, Mass.: Belknap Press, 2007.

Kupperman, Karen O. *Roanoke: The Abandoned Colony.* Lanham, Md.: Rowman & Littlefield, 2007.

Lepore, Jill. *Encounters in the New World: A History in Documents.* New York: Oxford University Press, 2003.

Library of Congress. "Colonial America (1492–1763)." Available online. URL: http://www.americaslibrary.gov/cgi-bin/page.cgi/jb/colonial.

Lovejoy, Paul E. *Transformations in Slavery: A History of Slaves in Africa.* Cambridge: Cambridge University Press, 2000.

MacQuarrie, Kim. *The Last Days of the Incas.* New York: Simon & Schuster, 2007.

Marcovitz, Hal. *Vasco Nuñez De Balboa and the Discovery of the South Sea.* New York: Chelsea House, 2001.

Mariner's Museum, Newport News, Virginia. "Age of Exploration." Available online. URL: http://www.mariner.org/educationalad/ageofedx/.

Marquette, Jacques. *Marquette's First Voyage, 1673–1677: Travels and Explorations of the Jesuit Missionaries in New France.* Oaksdale, Wash.: Ye Galleon Press, 2001.

Marrin, Albert. *The Sea King: Sir Francis Drake and His Times.* New York: Atheneum, 1995.

McCarthy, Pat. *The Thirteen Colonies from Founding to Revolution in American History.* Berkeley Heights, N.J.: Enslow Publishers, 2004.

Miller, Jake. *The Lost Colony of Roanoke.* New York: PowerKids Press, 2005.

Miller, Lee. *Mystery of the Lost Colony.* New York: Scholastic, 2007.

Milner, George R. *The Moundbuilders: Ancient Peoples of Eastern North America.* New York: Thames & Hudson, 2005.

Morganelli, Adriana. *Samuel de Champlain: From New France to Cape Cod.* New York: Crabtree Books, 2005.

Newitt, Malyn. *A History of Portuguese Overseas Expansion.* New York: Routledge, 2005.

Otfinoski, Steven. *Vasco Nunez De Balboa: Explorer of the Pacific.* New York: Benchmark Books, 2004.

Paige, Joy. *Sir Francis Drake: Circumnavigator of the Globe and Privateer for Queen Elizabeth.* New York: Rosen Publishing, 2002.

Parker, Geoffrey. *The Grand Strategy of Philip II.* New Haven, Conn.: Yale University Press, 2000.

Parkman, Francis. *La Salle and the Discovery of the Great West.* New York: Modern Library, 1999.

Philbrick, Nathaniel. *Mayflower: A Story of Courage, Community, and War.* New York: Penguin, 2007.

Rietburgen, Piet. *A Short History of the Netherlands.* Langley, B.C.: Vanderheide Publishing, 2004.

Russell, Peter. *Prince Henry "the Navigator": A Life.* New Haven, Conn.: Yale University Press, 2000.

Sakurai, Gail. *The Jamestown Colony.* New York: The Children's Press, 1997.

Sanders, William. *Conquest—Hernando de Soto and the Indians: 1539–1543.* Rockville, Md.: Wildside Press, 2004.

Sandler, Corey. *Henry Hudson: Dreams and Obsession: The Tragic Legacy of the New World's Least Understood Explorer.* New York: Citadel, 2007.

Saunders, Nicholas J., and Tony Allan. The *Aztec Empire: Excavating the Past.* Portsmouth, N.H.: Heinemann Library, 2004.

Schultz, Eric B., and Michael J. Tougias. *King Philip's War: The History and Legacy of America's Forgotten War.* Woodstock, Vt.: Countryman Press, 2000.

Smallwood, Stephanie E. *Saltwater Slavery: A Middle Passage from Africa to American Diaspora.* Cambridge, Mass.: Harvard University Press, 2007.

Somerville, Barbara A. *Empire of the Inca.* New York: Facts On File, 2004.

Sonnenborn, Liz. *Samuel de Champlain.* London: Franklin Watts, 2002.

Stanford University. "Stanford Encyclopedia of Philosophy." Available online. URL: http://plato.stanford.edu/entries/colonialism/.

Taylor, Alan. *American Colonies: The Settling of North America.* New York: Penguin, 2006.

Taylor, Yuval. *Growing Up in Slavery: Stories of Young Slaves as Told By Themselves.* Chicago: Lawrence Hill, 2007.

Tormey, James. *John Rolfe of Virginia.* Silver Spring, Md.: Beckham Publications, 2006.

University of Calgary. "European Voyages of Exploration." Available online. URL: http://www.ucalgary.ca/aplied_history/tutor/eurvoya/

Waldman, Carl. *Atlas of the North American Indian.* New York: Facts On File, 2008.

Whitelaw, Nancy. *Queen Isabella: And the Unification of Spain.* Greensboro, N.C.: Morgan Reynolds, 2004.

Wilcox, Charlotte. *The Iroquois.* Minneapolis, MN: Learner, 2006.

Worth, Richard. *Voices from Colonial America: New France, 1534–1763.* Washington, D.C.: National Geographic Children's Press, 2007.

Index

Page numbers in **boldface** indicate topics covered in depth in the A to Z section of the book.

A

abolition, 80
abolitionists, 80
agriculture, 11, 54, 55, 59–60, 77, 93
Alaska, 77
Albany Plan of Union, 33–34
alliances, 15
allies, 10, 16, 32, 84
American Revolution, 10, 72
Anglican Church, 4, 6, 88–89, 92
annexation, 58, 63
Appalachian Mountains, **9–10**
archaeologists, 23
autonomy, 68, 73
Aztec empire, 7, **10–13**, 56

B

balance of trade, 52
Balboa, Vasco Nuñez de, **12–15**, 84
Baltimore, Cecil Calvert, Second Lord, 92
Baltimore, George Calvert, First Lord, 92
bankruptcy, 41
Bering, Vitus, 76
blacks, 3. *See also* slavery and the slave trade
booty, 28
Brazil, 80, 84, 96
British crown, 33
British North America Act (1867), 73
broadsheets, 41
buffer states, 92
business organizations, 42

C

Cabot, John, 26–27, 75
Canada, 15–16, 31
Cape of Good Hope, 21
Carolinas, 92
Cartier, Jacques, 31, 61, 72
cash crop, 43, 88, 95
Catholic Church, 29, 66, 92
ceded, 34
Champlain, Samuel de, **15–16**, 31, 62, 72, 99
Charles I, 90, 92
Charles II, 64–65, 89, 91
Charles V, 11, 22, 44
charter, 28, 38, 40, 75, 76, 92, 100, 103–4
Church of England, 4, 6, 88–89, 92
circumnavigation, 25, 47
Colbert, Jean-Baptiste, 53, 62
colonial era, 52, 65
colonies, 27, 47, 59, 65, 67
colonists, 1, 9, 24, 32, 39, 41, 67, 71–72, 78, 80, 84, 87, 100, 104
Columbus, Christopher, 11, **16–21**, 29–30, 65, 83
confederation, 59
Connecticut, 90–91
conquistadors, 11, 30, 36, 56, 65, 84
Cortés, Hernán, 7, 11–13, 84
Counter-Reformation, 84
Cuba, 18, 19, 22–23, 30

D

Da Gama, Vasco, **21–22**, 71
Dare, Virginia, 28, 75

De Soto, Hernando, **22–24**
Delaware, 91
dependencies, 1
Dias, Bartholomeu, 17, 21, 71
disease, 7, **24–25**, 84
Dominion of New England, 59
Drake, Sir Francis, **25–26**, 75
drawn and quartered, 46
Dutch East India Company, 57
Dutch West India Company, 57–58, 63

E

Eastern Woodlands culture, 54–56
economies of scale, 53
Edward VI, 27
Elizabeth I, 25, 27–28, 75
England, **26–29**
  early explorations, 26–27
  as European power, 27–29
  mercantilism, 52–53
  Native American relations with, 71
  Seven Years' War, 10, 32–34
  slave trade, 78, 80
  Spanish naval war, 25–26
  thirteen colonies, 2–7
epidemic disease, 24–25
equator, 19, 71
exports, 29, 39, 52

F

famine, 37, 39
fathoms, 49